Maths Dictionary

Kay Gardner

Published by HarperCollins*Publishers* Limited
77-85 Fulham Palace Road
Hammersmith
London
W6 8JB

www.**Collins**Education.com
Online support for schools and colleges

HarperCollins*Publishers* Limited 2002
First published 2002

Reprinted 10 9 8 7 6 5 4

ISBN 0 00 713059 7

British Library Cataloguing in Publication Data
A Catalogue record for this publication is available from the British Library

Designer   Sylvia Tate
Illustrators   Stuart Perry, Stephanie Strickland
Cover Designer   Susi Martin
Cover Illustrator   Tim Archbold
Numeracy Consultant   Lucy Simonds

Printed in Great Britain by Scotprint

How to Use This Book

To make the best use of this book, you will need to know what is in it. A complete list of the words starts on the next page. It is a good idea to start by looking up some words you do know. Dip into the book and find your way around it.

This book is more than a dictionary of maths words. It gives the spellings and meanings of words, but it also contains a lot of useful examples and reminders.

If you look up a word it will always explain what it means and sometimes it will tell you where to look for more information.

This book will not teach you how to do maths, but it should help you to understand words you are not sure of and to remember things that you have forgotten.

main headword   plural or other forms   guideword

pronunciation

alphabet line

cross-references (related words)

definition (some entries start with a simple explanation and continue with more advanced information)

This entry continues over the page

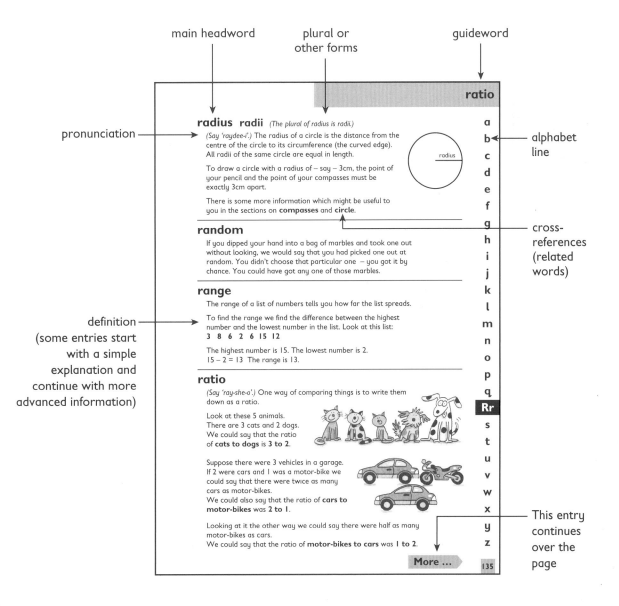

ratio

radius radii *(The plural of radius is radii.)*

(Say 'raydee-i'.) The radius of a circle is the distance from the centre of the circle to its circumference (the curved edge). All radii of the same circle are equal in length.

To draw a circle with a radius of – say – 3cm, the point of your pencil and the point of your compasses must be exactly 3cm apart.

There is some more information which might be useful to you in the sections on **compasses** and **circle**.

radius

random

If you dipped your hand into a bag of marbles and took one out without looking, we would say that you had picked one out at random. You didn't choose that particular one – you got it by chance. You could have got any one of those marbles.

range

The range of a list of numbers tells you how far the list spreads.

To find the range we find the difference between the highest number and the lowest number in the list. Look at this list:
3 8 6 2 6 15 12

The highest number is 15. The lowest number is 2.
15 − 2 = 13 The range is 13.

ratio

(Say 'ray-she-o'.) One way of comparing things is to write them down as a ratio.

Look at these 5 animals.
There are 3 cats and 2 dogs.
We could say that the ratio of **cats to dogs** is **3 to 2**.

Suppose there were 3 vehicles in a garage.
If 2 were cars and 1 was a motor-bike we could say that there were twice as many cars as motor-bikes.
We could also say that the ratio of **cars to motor-bikes** was **2 to 1**.

Looking at it the other way we could say there were half as many motor-bikes as cars.
We could say that the ratio of **motor-bikes to cars** was **1 to 2**.

a b c d e f g h i j k l m n o p q **Rr** s t u v w x y z

More ...

135

Contents

Aa
b
c
d
e
f
g
h
i
j
k
l
m
n
o
p
q
r
s
t
u
v
w
x
y
z

a.m. (am)

This stands for ante meridiem – Latin words meaning before midday. 5am means 5 o'clock in the morning. It is shown as 05:00 on the twenty-four hour clock.

(5**pm** (post meridiem) means 5 o'clock after midday. 5 o'clock in the afternoon.)

If you want to know more about this, look up **time** or the **twenty-four hour clock**.

abacus   *(The plural of abacus can be abacuses or abaci.)*

An abacus is a counting frame. It has wires or rods fixed across it and beads that can slide along them.

A spike abacus has spikes or rods fixed into a base. Discs or beads can be put on or taken off each spike.

Some abacuses have rails curved over like arches. You can bring forward the number of beads or discs you need and slide all the others over the top out of the way.
You can use an abacus with three spikes – or arches – to represent hundreds, tens and units (ones).

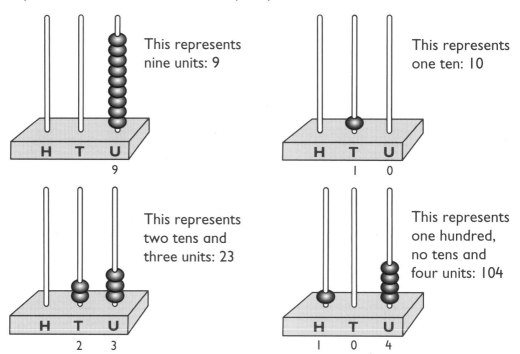

This represents nine units: 9

This represents one ten: 10

This represents two tens and three units: 23

This represents one hundred, no tens and four units: 104

acute angle

An acute angle is an angle which is less than 90°.
If you want to know more about this, look up **angles**.

add addition

Addition is counting up or finding the total of two or more numbers. We often call it adding up or adding on.

Count up   3 + 2 = 5

+ is the sign we use for words that mean add.
= is the equals sign. We also use it to mean 'is the same as' or 'makes.'
We might say 3 add 2 equals 5 or 3 add 2 makes 5.

You need to add for all of these examples.

3 *add* 4.   →   3 + 4 = 7

Add 2 *to* 2.   →   2 + 2 = 4

Add 6 *and* 4. →   6 + 4 = 10

3, 6 and 2, *how many altogether?*   →   3 + 6 + 2 = 11

What do 3 *and* 7 *make?*   →   3 + 7 = 10

Find the sum of 3 *and* 10. →   3 + 10 = 13

5 *plus* 4.   →   5 + 4 = 9

Total means count up – or add up – the whole lot.
You add to find the total number, total cost, total amount, total weight and so on.

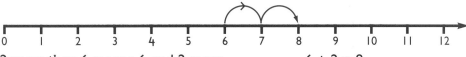

2 *more than* 6 means 6 and 2 more.   6 + 2 = 8

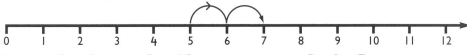

Increase 5 *by* 2 means 5 and 2 more.   5 + 2 = 7

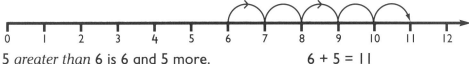

5 *greater than* 6 is 6 and 5 more.   6 + 5 = 11

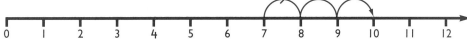

What must you add to 7 *to make* 10?   7 + 3 = 10

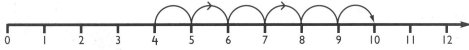

You have 4 badges.
How many more do you need *to make* 10?   4 + 6 = 10

Aa

b

c

d

e

f

g

h

i

j

k

l

m

n

o

p

q

r

s

t

u

v

w

x

y

z

adjacent

We hear about adjacent houses, adjacent gardens, adjacent angles, adjacent sides of a shape. Things which are next to each other are adjacent. They are adjoining.

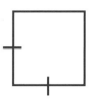

These two sides are adjacent

adjust adjustment

If you adjust something you change it a little bit. You might adjust something to make it fit better – or you might make an adjustment to an answer you've given or an estimate you've made. To add 9 to 23, for example, you might add 10 to 23 and then adjust it by taking 1 away.

altogether

Look at these buns.

4 + 1 + 2 = 7
There are 7 buns altogether.
To find out how many there are altogether you add them all up.

Look at these coins.

To find out how much it is altogether you add them all up.
10p + 5p + 2p = 17p
Altogether it comes to 17p.

amount

A price ticket tells us the amount that something costs.

It tells us **how much** it costs.
At the check-out we are told the amount that we have to pay for our shopping.
We are told how much to pay.

If we talk about the amount we can carry – or the amount we can fit into a space – we mean how much we can carry – or how much we can fit in.

analogue clock

An analogue clock has a face with 'hands' that turn round to point to the time.
(A digital clock doesn't have any hands. The numbers change to show us what the time is.)
Look up **time** if you want to know more about it.

angles

An angle is a measurement of turn. Angles are measured in degrees. To measure an angle we measure the amount of turn from the position of one line to the other.

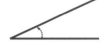

Think of an opening door. At first it is open a tiny amount and the angle is very small. The wider it opens, the larger the angle becomes.

The hands of a clock turn through angles as they go round. The minute hand goes in a complete circle in one hour.
A complete turn like that is measured as 360 degrees. We write it as 360°.

Half a turn is 180°
A quarter of a turn is 90°

Angles are measured using a **protractor**. (This is sometimes called an angle measurer.)

Right angles

Angles measuring 90° are called right angles. The angles at the corners of a square are all right angles. Right angles are often marked on diagrams by a small square.

Acute angles

Angles that are less than 90° are called acute angles. Acute angles are not the wide open ones, they measure less than the corner of a square. They are also more pointed looking and 'sharper' than other kinds of angle.

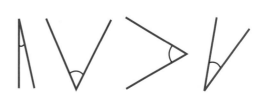

More ...

Obtuse angles

Angles that are more than 90° and less than 180° are called obtuse angles.

These are wide open angles.

Straight angles

Angles that measure exactly 180° are sometimes called straight angles.

Reflex angles

Angles that are larger than 180° are called reflex angles. Reflex angles are so wide open that they look as if the sides have been bent backwards!

anti-clockwise

Anti-clockwise means going round in the opposite direction to the hands of a clock.

clockwise   anti-clockwise

apex

The apex is the highest point of something; the top.

apparatus

You may talk about getting the apparatus out in P.E. You use some apparatus when you try things out in science. These are some of the pieces of apparatus that you may need to use in maths:

metre stick

balance

ruler

measuring cylinder

tape measure

pegs

pegboard

spinner

geo-strips

cubes

approximate

An approximate answer is not an exact answer – but it is 'near enough' for what we need. (It might be useful for you to read the sections on **approximately** and **approximation**.)

approximately

Approximately means nearly, round about, roughly. The sign we use for 'approximately equal to' is ≈ .

approximation

An approximation is an answer which is 'near enough'. Sometimes we don't need an exact answer. If a rough idea is good enough then we can use easy numbers. If we wanted to know roughly what 12 tickets would cost at 98p each we could say: 98p is nearly £1, so 12 x 98p is nearly 12 x £1.
Our answer would be approximately £12.

We may read in a newspaper that 15 000 people were at a special event. Nobody really believes that exactly 15 000 people were there. There might have been a few more. There might have been a few less. It doesn't matter to us. The reporter used 'round numbers' to give us an idea of the size of the crowd. That is an approximation too.

Approximations are sometimes needed to the nearest ten, to the nearest hundred, the nearest thousand and so on. Here are some examples:

To the nearest ten
138 is nearer to 140 than to 130. It is approximately 140.

To the nearest hundred
260 is nearer to 300 than to 200. It is approximately 300.

To the nearest thousand
12 040 is nearer to 12 000 than 13 000. It is approximately 12 000.

135 is halfway between 130 and 140. We would round this up to 140 if we needed the nearest ten . If you want to know more about this, look up **rounding**.

arc

Any part of the circumference of a circle is called an arc.

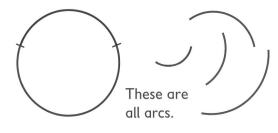

These are all arcs.

area

The **perimeter** is the distance all the way round something – the edge or the boundary. The **area** is the amount of surface space inside the perimeter. We measure it in squares. Of course all the squares must be the same size – all 1 square centimetre, or all 1 square metre for example.

This square is 1 cm long and 1 cm wide. Its area is 1 square centimetre. We write it as 1 cm² to save time.

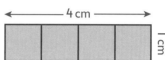

This shape measures 4 cm x 1 cm.
Its area is 4 cm².

There isn't always space on a page to draw shapes the full size. Often they are drawn smaller but they are labelled with the full size measurements.

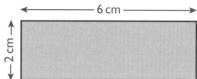

The area of this rectangle would be 12 square centimetres.
6 cm x 2 cm = 12 cm²

The quick way to find the area of a rectangle is to multiply the length by the breadth (width). But remember, the answer must always be a **square** measure. (It might be a number of mm² or cm² or m².)

The area = 5 cm x 3 cm = 15 cm²

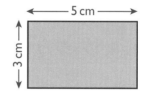

There are two ways of finding the area of a shape like this.

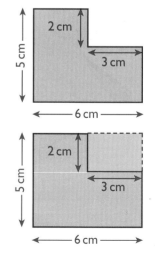

1 Build it up into the shape of a rectangle – see the dotted line. Find the area of the whole rectangle.

Next find the area of the blue rectangle: you don't want that bit! Take the area of the bit you don't want away from the area of the large rectangle – and you are left with the area of the bit you **do** want.

Area of large rectangle =   5 cm x 6 cm = 30 cm².
Area of small shaded rectangle = 2 cm x 3 cm = 6 cm².
Area of the shape we need =   30 cm² – 6 cm² = 24 cm².

b
c
d
e
f
g
h
i
j
k
l
m
n
o
p
q
r
s
t
u
v
w
x
y
z

2 The other way of finding the area of this shape is to split it up into two bits that you know how to deal with.

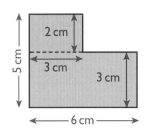

The top rectangle measures   2 cm x 3 cm = 6 cm^2.
The bottom rectangle measures   6 cm x 3 cm = 18 cm^2.
The area of the whole thing =   18 cm^2 + 6 cm^2 = 24 cm^2.

People sometimes forget how to find the areas of borders – but you tackle it in just the same way.

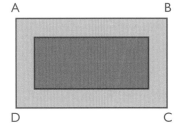

1 Find the area of the whole rectangle (ABCD).
2 Find the area of the middle bit.
3 Take the area of the middle bit away from the area of the whole thing. (Imagine the middle bit has a handle on it so that you can lift it out.) Then you are left with the area of the border.

The other way of tackling it is – as with the other awkward shape – to break it up into bits that you can manage.

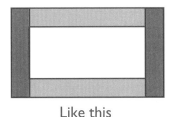  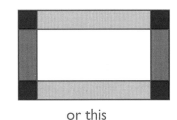

    Like this   or this   or this

You can't always choose which way you do it – it depends on which measurements you are given. Be a detective and use your clues!

arrange

If you arrange something you plan it or put it into order.
You organise it.
You might need to arrange some numbers in order or some shapes so that they fit together.

array

In maths an array is an arrangement of numbers or symbols in rows and columns.

If you look at this array you will see that there are 3 rows of fish. (Rows go across.)
There are 5 columns of fish. (Columns go from top to bottom.)

Aa
b
c
d
e
f
g
h
i
j
k
l
m
n
o
p
q
r
s
t
u
v
w
x
y
z

ascend

If you ascend the stairs you climb them — you go up. Ascending means climbing, going up.

ascending order

If you need to put a list of numbers in ascending order, the numbers will climb from the lowest to the highest. First find the lowest number, then the next lowest, then the next — and carry on until you get to the last number on the list. That will be the highest.

If you put 32, 1332, 5, 191, 16, into ascending order the list would become 5, 16, 32, 191, 1332. (Always check to make sure you haven't missed one out!)

average

There are three kinds of average that you will meet in maths: the mean, the median and the mode.

When we talk about average height, average age, average wages, batting average and so on, we are talking about the mean.

Here is an example about finding a batting average.
If ten batsmen each scored 10 runs, the average score would be 10: no one got more and no one got less. It would be very unusual though!

What if eight scored 10 each, one scored 0 and one scored 20?
The way to find this average is to add all the scores together to find the total, and then divide by the number of batsmen. The total score was:

$10 + 10 + 10 + 10 + 10 + 10 + 10 + 10 + 0 + 20 = 100$
There were ten batsmen: $100 \div 10 = 10$
The average is still 10. One batsman got more, one got less, but ten was the average number. The batsman scoring 0 was below average. The batsman scoring 20 was above average.

To find the average of anything like this you need a list of results, then:
1 Find the total (add up all the results).
2 Divide the total by the number of items — or people — in your list.
The answer is the average.

Here is another example:
In a test Ben got 22 marks, Tracy got 26, Ahmed got 29 and Jo got 31.

$22 + 26 + 29 + 31 = 108$
108 = total marks

Divide 108 by 4.
$108 \div 4 = 27$
27 = average mark

Remember: this kind of average is called the mean. You may find it useful to look up **mean** to see the example there.

Also: there are sections about the two other kinds of average under their own headings: **median** and **mode**. Look them up if you need to know about them.

axis axes *(The plural of axis is axes)*

(Say 'akseez'.) Imagine someone pushes a round stick right through an orange from top to bottom, and then spins the orange round the stick.

That stick is the axis.

An axis is a straight line through the middle of something. It can be a real line or an imaginary line. Things are arranged around it or turn around it. We say the world turns on its axis.

Axes on graphs
Every graph has two axes.

The horizontal axis is called the x-axis and the vertical axis is called the y-axis. (Remember: the x goes across.)

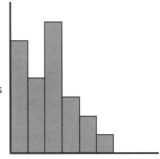

This is the vertical axis

This is the horizontal axis

An axis of symmetry
An axis of symmetry is a line or fold which divides a shape into two matching halves. (It is sometimes called the line of symmetry.)

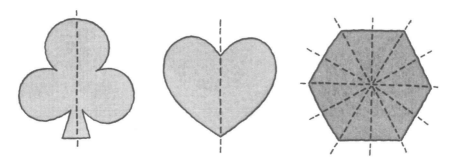

The dotted lines show the axes of symmetry.
(There are sections on **mirror-line**, **reflection** and **reflective symmetry** that might interest you.)

a
Bb
c
d
e
f
g
h
i
j
k
l
m
n
o
p
q
r
s
t
u
v
w
x
y
z

bar chart

A bar chart is a kind of graph where the information is shown in bars. Sometimes they are called bar graphs. Here is one which shows the favourite colours of children in a sports club.

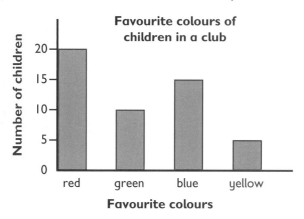

This chart shows that 20 children chose red, 10 chose green, 15 chose blue, and 5 chose yellow.
We can easily see that red was the most popular. Blue came next. Green came third and yellow was the least popular. We can also work out that there were 50 children altogether.

Sometimes the bars are drawn so that they are touching each other like these.

Sometimes the bars are drawn horizontally like this.

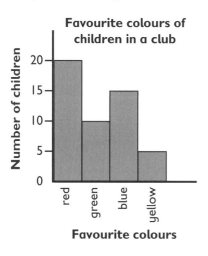

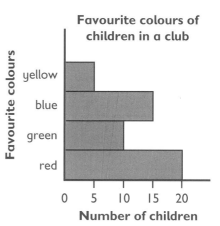

The important things to remember when you are drawing any kind of graph yourself, are:
1 to give your graph a heading or title so people know what it is all about
2 to label each axis so people can understand your information
3 to fit it on to your page so that it is as easy to see and understand as possible.

bar line chart

A bar line chart is very like a bar chart but lines are drawn to show the information instead of bars. Here is an example. It shows a girl's spelling test results for one month.

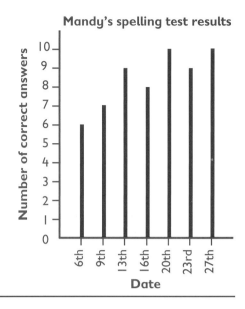

Mandy's spelling test results

base

A base is a foundation – something you can build on or use as a starting point. You use a base when you make a model. When we talk about the base – or the base line – of a triangle, the base of a cube or a pyramid and so on, the base is the bottom.

bills

There are lots of different kinds of bill but they all ask for money to be paid. If you have been given a shopping list and a price list you can work out what the bill should come to.
Look at this example:

	£
3 packets of buns @ 60p each cost (3 x 60p)	1.80
2 cakes @ 55p each cost (2 x 55p)	1.10
4 cans of drink @ 70p each cost (4 x 70p)	2.80
(Add to find the total cost.) Total cost =	£5.70

These are things that a lot of people forget:

1 If I kilogram costs 50p

$\frac{1}{2}$ kg costs ($\frac{1}{2}$ of 50p) = 25p $1\frac{1}{2}$ kg costs (50p + 25p) = 75p

2 There is sometimes a quick way of working prices out.
Here is an example.
Some plants cost 99p each.
Remember 99p is one penny less than £1.00.
1 plant would cost (£1.00 – 1p)   99p
2 plants would cost (£2.00 – 2p)   £1.98
3 plants would cost (£3.00 – 3p)   £2.97.

You may find the sections on **money** and **change** useful.

a
Bb
c
d
e
f
g
h
i
j
k
l
m
n
o
p
q
r
s
t
u
v
w
x
y
z

bisect

If we bisect something we divide it equally into two. The **bi** part of the word means two as it does in **bicycle**, **biplane**, **bifocal**. The **sect** bit comes from the same word as section. The diagonals of
— a square
— a rectangle
— a parallelogram
— and a rhombus
bisect each other.

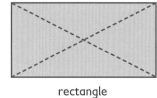
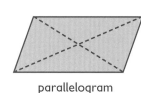
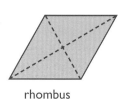

square   rectangle   parallelogram   rhombus

block graph

A block graph is a sort of chart which shows some information without using many words. It makes it very easy to understand. Here is one about the colours of sweets in a packet. Each block stands for one sweet.

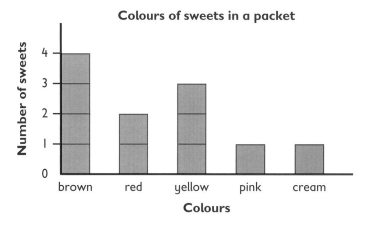

breadth

Breadth is the measurement across something from one side to the other. It is the same as width — it tells you how wide it is.

British Summer Time (BST)

Every year, sometime in March, we all put our clocks forward one hour. Then sometime in October we put them back. The aim is to make the best use of daylight and — although it does cover more than the summer season — it is called British Summer Time.

calculate

Calculate means work out. You might have to calculate the difference between two numbers for example, or the total cost of a day out.

calculation

If you make a calculation you work something out. 'Show your calculations' means show how you worked it out – show how you got your answer.

'Check your calculations' means check your working out – make sure you have got the right answer.

If you make a mental calculation, you think something out – you work it out in your head.

calculator

A calculator can do a lot of working out very quickly but you have to press the right keys to make it do the right work.

Some of the instruction leaflets that come with calculators are not very easy to understand. If you have one of these don't try to sort out too much at once – and don't give up.

Ask someone to help you get started and find out a bit at a time.

key: the keys are the buttons that you press to make the calculator work, e.g. the number keys, operation keys, decimal point key.

ON/CE: this key is used to switch on your calculator and also to clear an entry if you have keyed in the wrong thing. (NOTE: some calculators have separate **ON** and **Clear** keys.)

enter: if you enter something, you key it in.

operation keys: + – ÷ x These are the keys that do your addition, subtraction, division and multiplication.

display: the display shows what you key in – it displays it. At the end of the calculation it shows the answer.

= this is the key you press to get the result of your calculation.

Don't forget to clear the display before you start a new calculation.

memory: this key is for storing a number that you want to use later in your calculation.

MRC: press this key to display the number stored in memory. With some calculators you press this key twice to clear the memory. Some calculators have a separate **MC** (memory clear) key.

sign change: some calculators have a +/– key that you can use to change the sign from positive to negative (or the other way round.)

constant function: you may be able to use a constant key if you want to keep repeating the same step – for example, multiplying by the same number over and over again.

More ...

a
b
Cc
d
e
f
g
h
i
j
k
l
m
n
o
p
q
r
s
t
u
v
w
x
y
z

When you are using a calculator use this plan of work.

1 Approximate: Get a rough idea of what the answer should be. Round about how many – or round about how much?

2 Calculate: Use the real numbers to work out what the real answer is.

3 Check: Check to make sure that your answer is right. It is very easy to make mistakes when you are pressing keys quickly. If you have a rough idea of what the result should be, you can stop yourself from giving a silly answer.

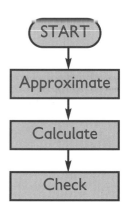

START → Approximate → Calculate → Check

Look at this example: 5·36 x 4

Approximate: 5 x 4 = 20
5·36 x 4 will be a bit more than 20.

Calculate: Answers of 2·144 or 214·4 could not possibly be right. 21·44 sounds much more likely.

Check: You could use the calculator to try 4 x 5·36 to see if that comes to 21·44 as well. Another way to check would be to try 21·44 ÷ 4 to see if that took you back to 5·36 again.

Check the way you are using the calculator sometimes. Work through some examples where you are sure you know the answers.

There is one more thing that you must be careful about. If you have to work out something like 3 + (2 x 10) anything in brackets must be worked out first. 3 + (2 x 10) = 3 + 20 = 23
A lot of calculators don't have brackets – they work out each piece of the calculation in the order you put it in.
They would calculate 3 + 2 x 10 = 5 x 10 = 50.
To get the **right** answer you would have to give the calculator the right piece of work to do first. You would put in the piece in brackets first: 2 x 10 **then** + 3 . Then you would get 23.

calendar

A calendar is a collection of tables showing the days, weeks and months of a year.

| 24 hours | = | 1 day |
| 7 days | = | 1 week |

2 weeks, when one is straight after the other, are sometimes called a fortnight.

June

Sun	Mon	Tue	Wed	Thu	Fri	Sat
			1	2	3	4
5	6	7	8	9	10	11
12	13	14	15	16	17	18
19	20	21	22	23	24	25
26	27	28	29	30		

There is one week from one Sunday to the next Sunday. There is one week from one Monday to the next Monday, and so on. It is easy to count up the weeks by looking down the columns of a calendar.

| 52 weeks = 1 year |
| 12 months = 1 year |

There is one year from one January to the next. There is one year from one February to the next, from one March to the next and so on. There is one year from one birthday to the next.
This rhyme helps us to remember how many days there are in each month:

30 days hath September,
April, June and November.
All the rest have 31,
Except February alone,
And this has 28 days clear,
But 29 in each leap year.

There are   365 days in 1 year
           366 days in 1 **leap** year
(Look up **leap year** if you want to know more about that.)

---

cancel cancelling

In maths we often cancel when we can divide the **numerator** and the **denominator** of a fraction by the same number. This doesn't change the value of the fraction but it gives us smaller numbers to work with.

$$\frac{4}{16} \quad = \quad \frac{2}{8} \quad = \quad \frac{1}{4}$$

These are examples of cancelling:

$$\frac{4}{16} = \frac{\cancel{4} \times 1}{\cancel{4} \times 4} = \frac{1}{4} \qquad \frac{2}{8} = \frac{\cancel{2} \times 1}{\cancel{2} \times 4} = \frac{1}{4} \qquad \frac{9}{12} = \frac{\cancel{3} \times 3}{\cancel{3} \times 4} = \frac{3}{4}$$

Here are some more.

$$\frac{\cancel{3}^{1}}{\cancel{6}_{2}} = \frac{1}{2} \qquad \frac{\cancel{6}^{2}}{\cancel{9}_{3}} = \frac{2}{3} \qquad \frac{\cancel{10}^{2}}{\cancel{15}_{3}} = \frac{2}{3}$$

We 'cancel' when we simplify a fraction – or reduce a fraction to its lowest terms – and sometimes when we multiply or divide fractions. Remember: the numerator and the denominator must be divided by the same number. We call it a **common factor**. If you have forgotten about this, look up **fractions** (the part under **cancelling**).

capacity

Capacity is the amount that something will hold.
We talk about:
– the capacity of a car boot
– the capacity of a freezer, or a watering can,
– the capacity of a bucket, or a jug and so on.

Containers
Containers are used for holding things. Their capacity is the amount that they can hold – or contain. These are all examples of containers:

If something is **full** it is holding as much as it can. People sometimes say it is **full up** or **full to capacity**.

empty   half full   full

A measuring cylinder can be very useful for measuring amounts of liquid.

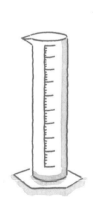

Capacity can be measured in different ways. The amount of liquid that something can hold is usually measured in litres (l) or millilitres (ml).

1000 ml = 1 litre   500 ml = $\frac{1}{2}$ litre

Sometimes centilitres are used.
100 centilitres (cl) = 1 litre (l)

You may still see the imperial units of pints and gallons.
(8 pints = gallon)

1 litre is about $1\frac{3}{4}$ pints (1·75 pints)   1 gallon is about $4\frac{1}{2}$ litres (4·5 litres)

Carroll diagrams

Carroll diagrams are a way of sorting things into groups.
You could sort out 12 7 3 21 8 9 20 2 into even numbers and numbers that are not even, like this:

even numbers	numbers that are not even
12	7
8	3
2	9
20	21

Carroll diagrams are very useful if you need to sort things out in two different ways.
Look at that list of numbers again.
Suppose you had to sort them two ways:
1 into even numbers and numbers that were not even
AND
2 into numbers that divide exactly by 3 and numbers that will not divide exactly by 3.
You could sort it out in a Carroll diagram like this:

	Even numbers	Numbers that are not even
Numbers that divide exactly by 3	12	3 9 21
Numbers that do not divide exactly by 3	8 2 20	7

When they are sorted out like this it is easy to see which numbers belong in which group.

Celsius centigrade

Celsius was a Swedish scientist and the Celsius temperature scale is named after him. °C stands for degrees Celsius.
(It is sometimes called **degrees centigrade**. The measuring scale is the same.)

0°C is the freezing point of water.
100°C is the boiling point of water.

A minus sign (–) before a number of degrees shows a number of degrees below zero.
– 5°C (minus 5 degrees Celsius) means 5° below zero.

a
b
Cc
d
e
f
g
h
i
j
k
l
m
n
o
p
q
r
s
t
u
v
w
x
y
z

centi-

Words beginning with centi- have something to do with a hundred.

centilitre

A centilitre is a metric measure of **capacity**. (How much something holds.)

100 cl = 1 litre (l)

1 centilitre (cl) = $\frac{1}{100}$ of a litre.

centimetre

A centimetre is a measurement of length in the metric system.

This line ▬▬ is one centimetre (cm) long.

100 cm = 1 metre (m)

1 cm is $\frac{1}{100}$ of a metre.

In the imperial measurements:

2·5 cm ($2\frac{1}{2}$ cm) is about 1 inch.

30 cm is about 1 foot.

century

A century is 100 years long.
We are now in the 21st century. 1918 is in the 20th century. 1837 is in the 19th century. This is not as silly as it sounds. The first hundred years of this time period went up to 100, the 2nd century went through the 100s, the 3rd century through the 200s and so on.

change

The word **change** has something to do with a difference of some kind.

1 You might change places with somebody – then you would be in a different place. Or your group might change over to some other work. Then you would be doing something different.

2 When we get change so that we can use a slot machine, we still have the same amount of money. It's just made up differently. We might get 5 ten pence pieces for a fifty pence piece.

3 Buying and selling is not quite the same. If we don't have exactly the right money to pay the shopkeeper for what we want, we give them a bit too much and they give us the change. The change is the difference between the price of what we are buying and the money we give the shopkeeper.

Here is an example.
We gave the shopkeeper 50p
The sweets we wanted to buy cost 40p
We got 10p change.
(50p – 40p = 10p)
You can always find the difference between two amounts by taking the smaller amount away from the bigger one.

Another way is 'counting on'.
40p + 10p = 50p. The change is 10p.
Shopkeepers sometimes count on from the price as they put your change into your hand.

| Shop price | | change | | | I gave |
| 35p | + | 10p | + | 5p | = | 50p |

I gave the shopkeeper 50p.
My change was 15p.

4 We also use the word **change** if we change something into something else. We might change centimetres into metres for example, or pints into litres. If you want to know more about changing things like this, look up **convert**.

circle

A circle is a round 2D shape. If you draw carefully round a 2p coin you have drawn a circle. A complete turn in a circle is 360 degrees (360°).

It is quite easy to draw circles using compasses. (Look up **compasses** if you have forgotten how to use them.)

You might want to look up some of these words. They are all to do with circles: **circumference**, **diameter**, **radius**, **semi-circle**, **quadrant**, **arc**.

circular

If something is circular it is round – shaped like a circle.

circumference

The circumference is the distance all the way round a circle: the boundary line.

u
b
Cc
d
e
f
g
h
i
j
k
l
m
n
o
p
q
r
s
t
u
v
w
x
y
z

classify

If you classify some information you sort it out into 'classes' or groups. You might classify some TV programmes into groups such as: Sport, Drama, Soaps, Documentaries, Quiz shows, Cartoons and so on. You would decide which classification each programme would come under. You might use a computer to collect and classify data (information) for a project.

Sometimes you may have to classify some numbers in a certain way – or some shapes according to their properties (numbers of equal sides, parallel sides, right angles and so on.)

Look up **properties** if you need to know more about that.

clockwise

Turning clockwise means going round in the same direction as the hands of a clock.

common denominator

The denominator is the bottom number of a fraction. It is the name of the fraction and tells us what sort it is. We can make it easier to add fractions together (or take one away from another) by making sure they have the same denominator.

2 fifths + 1 fifth = 3 fifths   4 fifths – 3 fifths = 1 fifth

$$\frac{2}{5} + \frac{1}{5} = \frac{3}{5} \qquad\qquad \frac{4}{5} - \frac{3}{5} = \frac{1}{5}$$

If we are dealing with **different kinds** of fractions we can change them to the same kind before we can add or subtract them. We find a denominator which will fit them all. It is common to them all and we call it a common denominator.

Look at $\frac{1}{2} + \frac{1}{4}$ We can change $\frac{1}{2}$ into quarters $\frac{1}{2} = \frac{2}{4}$ $\frac{2}{4} + \frac{1}{4} = \frac{3}{4}$

The common denominator is 4
4 will go into 4 exactly
2 will go into 4 exactly.

For $\frac{1}{3} + \frac{2}{9}$ 9 could be the common denominator
                   3 will go into 9 exactly (3 lots of 3 make 9)
                   9 will go into 9 exactly (1 lot of 9 makes 9)
                   Both fractions could be ninths.

For $\frac{1}{2} + \frac{1}{3} + \frac{5}{6}$ 6 could be the common denominator
2 will go into 6 exactly (3 times)
3 will go into 6 exactly (twice)
All three fractions could be sixths.
Look up **fractions** if you want to know more about this.

compare

You compare things when you are asked questions like these:
Which is the higher price 35p or 53p?
Which is the shorter journey 101 km or 110 km?
Which is the greatest number 42 402 365 102?
You need to compare the numbers in a list if you have to put them in a certain order. (Look up **ordering** if you need to know more about that.)
When we are just comparing two things we might say that one is bigger than the other one – or that one is smaller than the other one.
Sometimes we may be comparing three or more things.

Look at this box.   This one is bigger.   This is the biggest.

Here are some words for comparing two things:
(You do not **always** need the word 'than.')
smaller (than)   less (than)   fewer (than)
bigger (than)   greater (than)   more (than)   larger (than)

shorter (than)   narrower (than)   shallower (than)   lower (than)
longer (than)   wider (than)   deeper (than)   higher (than)   taller (than)

lighter (than)   thinner (than)   younger (than)   earlier (than)   nearer (than)
heavier (than)   thicker (than)   older (than)   later (than)   further (than)

Here are some words for comparing three or more things:
smallest   least   fewest
biggest   greatest   most   largest

shortest   narrowest   shallowest   lowest
longest   widest   deepest   highest   tallest

lightest   thinnest   youngest   earliest   nearest   closest
heaviest   thickest   oldest   latest   furthest

There are signs that we can use in maths for greater than and less than:
20 **>** 5 means 20 is greater than (or more than) 5.
 5 **<** 20 means 5 is less than 20.
Think of the sign as a hungry mouth – it always opens towards the larger amount!
(If you compare things and find that they are equal – or worth the same – you can use the = sign of course.)

compass

A compass is used for finding direction. It has a magnetised needle in the middle that can swing to and fro freely, and it points in the direction of north.

If you move the compass round until the needle is exactly over the direction marked N (or north) you can find all the other directions. The compass points we use most are north, south, east and west (N, S, E and W).

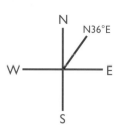

In between those points come north-east, south-east, south-west and north-west (NE, SE, SW, NW).

(There are more points of the compass in between those, but most people don't need to use them very often.)

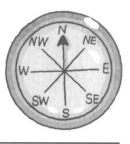

compasses

(We talk about a pair of compasses like a pair of scissors.)

Compasses are used for drawing circles and parts of circles (**arcs**). If you need a reminder about using them, read this:

1 Before you start to use compasses make sure you have a good point on your pencil.

2 Make sure that the compass point and the pencil point are level and screw the pencil in so that it doesn't wobble.

3 Open the compasses and put the compass point where you want the middle of your circle to be. (Make sure the point doesn't go into the table.)

4 Hold the compasses near the top so you don't squeeze the sides together.

5 Keep the point of the compasses still and swing the pencil leg first in one direction then in the other so that the pencil point can mark out the circle.

The point of the compasses goes at the centre of the circle and the pencil point marks out the **circumference**.
The distance between the centre of the circle and the circumference is called the **radius**.

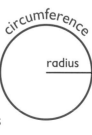

To draw a circle with a radius of 3 cm, make sure that the compass point and the pencil point are exactly 3 cm apart before you start. Use a ruler to measure the gap.

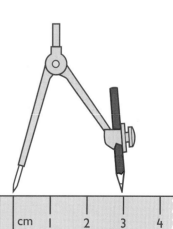

complete

We use this word in two ways:

1 Complete meaning **finish**:
If you are told to complete something you have to finish it.
For example, *Complete this calculation:* $5 + \square = 12$ means that you have to finish it. You have to find the missing number.
If your work is complete, it is finished. (If it is **incomplete** something is missing. You haven't finished!)

2 Complete meaning **whole**:
If you have a complete set of stickers you have the whole set.
If you make a complete turn you turn the whole way round. You end up facing the same way as you did when you started.

concave

Concave means curving inwards, like a hollow.
(Think of con**cave**.) The opposite is **convex**.

concave   convex

concentric

These circles are concentric.
Concentric circles have the same centre.

cone

A cone is a 3D shape with a flat circular base.
Its top is pointed. Its sides are curved. The top may be called the vertex or the apex.

congruent

Congruent means exactly the same size and shape.
Two circles are congruent if they have the same radius.
They would fit exactly on top of each other.
These triangles are congruent.

consecutive

Things that are consecutive follow on after each other. If it rained on Monday, Tuesday, Wednesday and Thursday one week, we might say that it had rained on four consecutive days.

Consecutive numbers follow on straight after each other too.
19 20 21 22 23   are consecutive numbers.
32 34 36 38   are consecutive even numbers.

constant

If people grumble about a constant noise they mean a noise which goes on all the time and never stops.

In maths something is called a constant if it has the same value all the time and never changes.

Sometimes a letter is used to stand for an amount in an equation. If it just stands for one amount which stays the same, it is called a constant. If it can stand for any one of a whole range of amounts it is called a variable.

A constant stays constantly the same. A variable can change.

construct constructions

If you construct something you build it or put it together. You might construct a model boat or plane, a 3D shape out of a piece of cardboard, or a plan on a sheet of paper.

Constructions may also be drawings which are built up carefully and accurately. A pair of compasses, a ruler, a sharp pencil, a set square or a protractor may be needed. The drawing of a triangle to exact measurements is one example of a construction.

To construct a triangle with sides of 5 cm, 4 cm and 3 cm:

1 Draw a line exactly 5 cm long. If you want it to be the base line leave space above it for the rest of the triangle.

2 Open your compasses so that the compass point and pencil point are exactly 4 cm apart.

3 With the compass point at A and the compasses open 4 cm, draw an arc. Any point on this arc must be 4 cm away from A.

4 Open the compasses 3 cm exactly.

5 With the compass point at B draw an arc to cut the arc you drew from A. The point where the two arcs cut each other must be 4 cm from A and 3 cm from B. Call this point C.

6 Join AC and BC.

(The sections on **protractor** or **nets** might be of interest to you as well.)

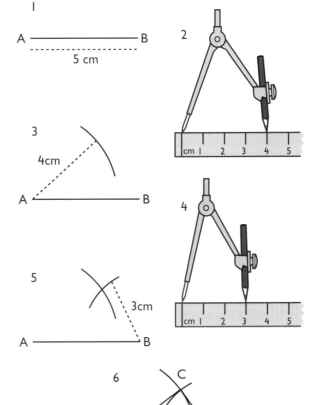

continue

If you continue to do something you keep on doing it. If you continue to use the same pattern you keep repeating it.

If something has been started and you are told to continue it, look carefully to see what has been done before and then try to carry on in the same way.

conversion

A conversion is a change from one thing to another. If we make a conversion we convert something into something else.

If you want to know more about this, read **convert**. (There is an example of a conversion graph there as well.)

convert

When you convert something you change it from one thing to another. If you are going to another country you may have to convert some of your money to the kind of money that is used there: into US dollars for example, or Swiss francs.

If you want to know how far away a place is in kilometres and your map shows distances in miles you will have to convert the miles into kilometres. (5 miles are about 8 kilometres.)

Changing units

If you convert £1 to pence you will have 100p. It will be worth the same but you will have more coins. If you convert £2 to pence you will have 200p (2 x 100p).

If you convert your units to some that are bigger – or worth more – you will get a smaller number of the bigger units. If you convert 200 pence into one pound coins, for example, you divide the number of pence by 100. For every 100p you would get 1 one pound coin. For 200 pence you would get 2 one pound coins.

To convert pence to pounds divide by 100
pounds to pence multiply by 100

To convert mm to cm divide by 10
cm to m divide by 100
m to km divide by 1000

10 mm = 1 cm
100 cm = 1 m
1000 m = 1 km

To convert cm to mm multiply by 10
m to cm multiply by 100
km to m multiply by 1000

To convert minutes to hours divide by 60
hours to minutes multiply by 60

60 minutes = 1 hour

More ...

a
b
Cc
d
e
f
g
h
i
j
k
l
m
n
o
p
q
r
s
t
u
v
w
x
y
z

Look up **percentages** if you want a reminder about converting percentages and fractions or decimals.
If you want to convert a number of units to a different kind – miles to kilometres for example, it can be useful to make a conversion graph.
Look at this one on the right.

Once you have worked out a few of the points and joined them up, you can read off a whole lot more.

20 miles is about 32 kilometres
80 kilometres is about 50 miles

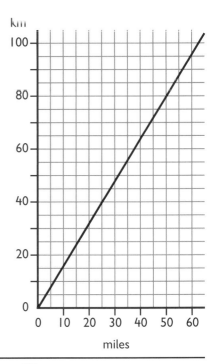

km

miles

convex

Convex means curving like the **outside** of a dome. The opposite is **concave**.

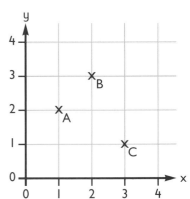

concave   convex

co-ordinates

Co-ordinates are numbers or letters which help us to find the exact position of something. They are often used on maps, graphs and charts.

Look at the diagram on the right. The lines going across are **horizontal** and the lines going straight up are **vertical**.

We call the vertical axis the y-axis and the horizontal axis the x-axis. (Remember, the **x** goes **across**.)
We always write the **x-axis** co-ordinate **first**.
The numbers here start from 0, 0 in the bottom left corner.
The point at A is 1 square along and 2 squares up.
We write this as (1, 2)
The co-ordinates of A are (1, 2)
The point at B is 2 squares along and 3 squares up.
We write this as (2, 3)
The co-ordinates of B are (2, 3)
To find a point on this grid, we look **along** and then **up**.
The co-ordinates (3, 1) lead us to the point at C.

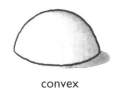

Co-ordinates can use negative numbers as well as positive ones.
The axes have to be extended beyond the zeros (like number lines) to include these.

Look at this grid. It shows negative numbers on the x-axis.

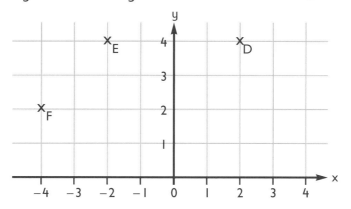

The point at D is (2, 4).
The co-ordinates of D are (2, 4).
The point at E is (−2, 4).
The co-ordinates of E are (−2, 4).
The co-ordinates (−4, 2) lead us to the point at F.

The next grid shows the negative numbers on the y-axis as well.
For these negative numbers we look along, then down.

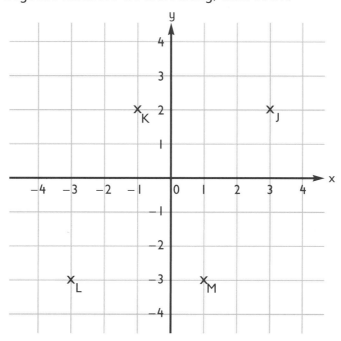

The co-ordinates of J are (3, 2).
The co-ordinates of K are (−1, 2).
The co-ordinates of L are (−3, −3).
The co-ordinates (1, −3) lead us to the point at M.

a
b
Cc
d
e
f
g
h
i
j
k
l
m
n
o
p
q
r
s
t
u
v
w
x
y
z

correct

1 If something is correct it is right. If something is incorrect it is wrong. If you correct it you put it right. You have made a correction.

2 If you have been using **decimals** you might need to give an answer 'correct to a number of places.' This is a kind of **rounding**.
If you had to write 6·42 correct to 1 decimal place you would only have 1 digit after the decimal point. You would round it down to 6·4.
If you had to write 6·48 correct to 1 decimal place you would round it up to 6·5 because 6·48 is nearer to 6·5 than to 6·4.
Look up **rounding** if you want to know more about that.

cost

The cost of something is the amount you have to pay for it. It is the **price** you have to pay.
If you want to buy something you need to know how much it costs.
It might be cheap – it might be good value. It might be dear – it might be too expensive.
The sections on **money**, **bills**, **change** or **discount** might interest you.

count counting

How many jam tarts are there?
How many sweets are there?
We count to find 'how many?'
When we haven't got any at all we have none.
We write 0. We call it zero.

Sometimes we use a **number line** for counting.

Count up to 12 from zero.

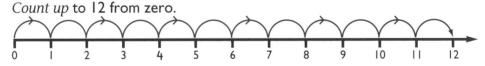

Count back from 12 to zero.

Count up to 12 *in twos*.

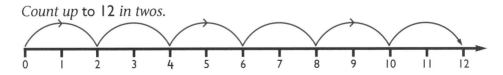

Count back from 12 to zero *in twos*.

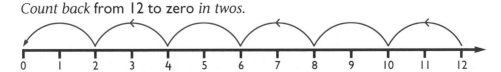

We can count up – or back – in threes … in fours … in fives … and so on.
We can start with any number and count on from there.
We can start from any number and count back from there.

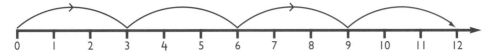

Now look back at the number line where we were counting up in twos.
We counted 2 4 6 8 10 12 …
If we count in twos we don't count every number. We started at zero and we didn't say 1, we said 2, we didn't say 3, we said 4, we didn't say 5, we said 6 and so on. This is called **counting every other number**.

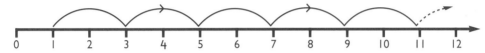

When we are counting every other number we don't have to start from two – we can start from anywhere.

Words and numbers for counting

zero	0	
one	1	▢
two	2	▢▢
three	3	▢▢▢
four	4	▢▢▢▢
five	5	▢▢▢▢▢
six	6	▢▢▢▢▢▢
seven	7	▢▢▢▢▢▢▢
eight	8	▢▢▢▢▢▢▢▢
nine	9	▢▢▢▢▢▢▢▢▢
ten	10	▢▢▢▢▢▢▢▢▢▢
eleven	11	▢▢▢▢▢▢▢▢▢▢ ▢
twelve	12	▢▢▢▢▢▢▢▢▢▢ ▢▢
thirteen	13	▢▢▢▢▢▢▢▢▢▢ ▢▢▢
fourteen	14	▢▢▢▢▢▢▢▢▢▢ ▢▢▢▢
fifteen	15	▢▢▢▢▢▢▢▢▢▢ ▢▢▢▢▢
sixteen	16	▢▢▢▢▢▢▢▢▢▢ ▢▢▢▢▢▢
seventeen	17	▢▢▢▢▢▢▢▢▢▢ ▢▢▢▢▢▢▢
eighteen	18	▢▢▢▢▢▢▢▢▢▢ ▢▢▢▢▢▢▢▢
nineteen	19	▢▢▢▢▢▢▢▢▢▢ ▢▢▢▢▢▢▢▢▢
twenty	20	▢▢▢▢▢▢▢▢▢▢ ▢▢▢▢▢▢▢▢▢▢
twenty-one	21	▢▢▢▢▢▢▢▢▢▢ ▢▢▢▢▢▢▢▢▢▢ ▢
twenty-two	22	▢▢▢▢▢▢▢▢▢▢ ▢▢▢▢▢▢▢▢▢▢ ▢▢
twenty-three	23	▢▢▢▢▢▢▢▢▢▢ ▢▢▢▢▢▢▢▢▢▢ ▢▢▢

More …

a
b

Cc

d
e
f
g
h
i
j
k
l
m
n
o
p
q
r
s
t
u
v
w
x
y
z

Saying and spelling

The numbers **up to twelve** all have quite different names –
and some of the spellings are surprising.
one sounds like wun.
two sounds like too.
four sounds like for.
eight sounds like the ate in late!

The 'teens' numbers

After 12 we get the **'teens' numbers**:
thirteen, fourteen, fifteen, sixteen, seventeen,
eighteen, nineteen.

After nineteen we start a pattern of words for counting that
goes on and on and on:
twenty, twenty-one, twenty-two, twenty-three, … and so on,
thirty, thirty-one, thirty-two, thirty-three, … and so on.

A hundred square

Look at this number square. You can
see the pattern of counting up to 100.
You can count across, row by row.
If you look down each column from top
to bottom you can see a pattern of
counting in tens – whichever number
you start from.

1	2	3	4	5	6	7	8	9	10
11	12	13	14	15	16	17	18	19	20
21	22	23	24	25	26	27	28	29	30
31	32	33	34	35	36	37	38	39	40
41	42	43	44	45	46	47	48	49	50
51	52	53	54	55	56	57	58	59	60
61	62	63	64	65	66	67	68	69	70
71	72	73	74	75	76	77	78	79	80
81	82	83	84	85	86	87	88	89	90
91	92	93	94	95	96	97	98	99	100

The words for counting the tens from
zero up to one hundred are:
zero ten twenty thirty forty
fifty sixty seventy eighty ninety
one hundred.

(Look at the word **forty**. Forty and the forty-something
words don't have the u in them like four and fourteen do.)

The words and numbers for counting up the hundreds from
zero to a thousand are:
zero one hundred two hundred three hundred
four hundred five hundred six hundred
seven hundred eight hundred nine hundred
one thousand.

0 100 200 300 400 500 600 700 800 900 1000

You might find it useful to look up **addition, subtraction,**
difference or **place value**.

cube

A cube is 3D. It is a square box shape.

It has 6 faces. (Four sides, a top and a bottom.) It is a special sort of cuboid: every face of a cube is a square. All of these squares are the same size: they are congruent. (That means exactly the same shape and size.)
A cube has 8 **vertices** (corners) and 12 edges.

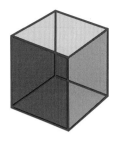

Look up **surface area** if you need a reminder about that.
Look up **volume** if you need to know about the volume of a cube.

cubic centimetre

A cube which is 1 centimetre long, 1 centimetre high, and 1 centimetre wide is called a cubic centimetre. We can write 1 cubic centimetre as 1 cm^3.

cubic numbers

1 cubed means 1 x 1 x 1.
It is written as 1^3.
1^3 = 1

2 cubed means 2 x 2 x 2.
It is written as 2^3.
2^3 = 8

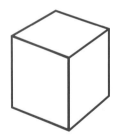

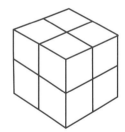

3 cubed means 3 x 3 x 3.
It is written as 3^3.
3^3 = 27

1 cubed = 1^3	It means 1 x 1 x 1	1^3 = 1
2 cubed = 2^3	It means 2 x 2 x 2	2^3 = 8
3 cubed = 3^3	It means 3 x 3 x 3	3^3 = 27
4 cubed = 4^3	It means 4 x 4 x 4	4^3 = 64
5 cubed = 5^3	It means 5 x 5 x 5	5^3 = 125 and so on.

These are cubic numbers:

1^3	2^3	3^3	4^3	5^3	and so on.
1	8	27	64	125	and so on.

a
b
Cc
d
e
f
g
h
i
j
k
l
m
n
o
p
q
r
s
t
u
v
w
x
y
z

cuboid

A cuboid is a 3D rectangular box shape. It has 6 faces (four sides, a top and a bottom).

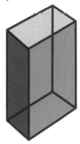

All the faces are rectangles. It is also a rectangular prism.
A cuboid has 8 **vertices** (corners) and 12 edges.
Look up **surface area** if you need a reminder about that.
Look up **volume** if you need to know about the volume of
a cuboid.

currency

Currency is the kind of money used in a country: for
example, U.S. dollars in America, Swiss francs in Switzerland,
or Japanese yen in Japan.

cylinder

A cylinder is a 3D shape. It is shaped like a roller. Its ends
are flat circles. These circles are parallel to each other.
A cylinder has the same diameter all through. It doesn't get
wider or narrower.

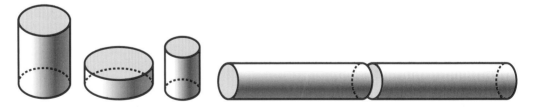

cylindrical

Cylindrical means shaped like a cylinder.

data

Data is information. It can include collections of facts in words or numbers – or a mixture of both.

It is often stored in files on paper or on computers. Data may be collected for a survey. You might make a survey of the TV programmes that people in your class watch for example. A survey like that helps to tell you what people think about something.

TV SURVEY

Did you watch TV last night?

☑ Yes   ☐ No

How many hours a day do you watch Monday to Friday?

☐ less than 2   ☐ 2-3   ☐ 4 or more

How many hours a day do you watch at weekends?

☐ less than 2   ☐ 2-3   ☐ 4-5
☐ 6 or more

What is your favourite type of programme?

☐ Cartoons   ☐ Comedy   ☐ News
☐ Soaps   ☐ Sport

☐ Other (*fill in*)

Sometimes people collect data by using a questionnaire.

They have a set of questions to ask and they collect the answers they get.

If there are a lot of possible answers they may have a list of them too. Sometimes each one has a box beside it so that they can quickly tick a box – or put a cross in it – when they get an answer.

Another way of collecting data is to ask people to vote about things.

Interpret

When you collect data you will find that it isn't always easy to use just as it is. You may have to sort it out and interpret it to show what it really means. You might make a table to show the results, or draw a **graph**, **pictogram** or a **pie chart**.

Interrogate

To interrogate is to question. If you have data stored in a computer database you can use it in different ways. Usually you enter a query – or fill in some boxes on the screen – when you want to use it. That starts a search of the data to find the information you need. This is sometimes called interrogating the database.

database

a
b
c
Dd
e
f
g
h
i
j
k
l
m
n
o
p
q
r
s
t
u
v
w
x
y
z

database

A database is used for storing data, often on a computer. This is done in an organised way so that data can be found and used quickly when it's needed.
(The section about **data** might be useful to you.

dates

Dates are often written in numbers.

25th December 1999 can be written as 25.12.99 – the 25th day of the 12th month in 1999.
5.11.02 means the 5th day of the 11th month in 2002, the 5th November 2002.

In Britain we always put the number of the day first, then the number of the month, then the year. Some digital watches show the days and months the other way round.
If you have one of these you must be careful not to get muddled up. Always write the day first!
It is useful to know your own **date of birth** in numbers – it is often needed for filling in forms.

Age: older or younger
If anyone's date of birth is before yours, they are older than you. They have been alive longer than you.
Someone born in 1990 is older than someone born in 1991.
Someone born in July 2000 is older than someone born in August 2000.
Anyone whose date of birth is after yours is younger than you. They were born after you so they haven't been here as long as you have.

Counting from one date to another
From 1st June to 2nd June is one whole day.
From 2nd May to 20th May there are 18 days.
You can count on from 2 to 20:
2 + 18 = 20
Or you can find the difference between the two dates:
20 – 2 = 18

Here is an example where the days run into different months.
How many days are there from 28th June to 4th July?
There are 30 days in June.
28th to 30th June = 2 days
30th June to 4th July = 4 days
Altogether 28th June to 4th July = 6 days.

a
b
c
Dd
e
f
g
h
i
j
k
l
m
n
o
p
q
r
s
t
u
v
w
x
y
z

(You might be able to use a calendar to help you.)

 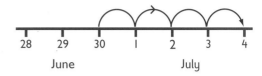

Sometimes you may need to work out a number of years.

Here is an example:
King Henry VIII ruled from 1509 to 1547. How many years was this?

One way to work it out is to count on from 1509 to 1547.
You could say:
From 1509 to 1510 is 1 year
1510 to 1547 is 37 years
Altogether 1509 to 1547 is 38 years.

Another way is to find the difference between the two dates by taking the earlier one away from the later one.
There are lots of ways of doing it!

days of the week

There are 7 days in a week. The days of the week are:

Monday Tuesday Wednesday Thursday Friday Saturday Sunday

Saturday and Sunday together are called the weekend.

decade

A decade is ten years.
Something which happened during the last decade happened during the last ten years.

decagon

A decagon is a 2D shape with ten straight sides and ten angles. If all the sides and angles are equal it is called a regular decagon.

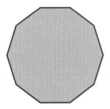

regular decagon

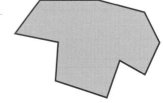

irregular decagon

a
b
c
Dd
e
f
g
h
i
j
k
l
m
n
o
p
q
r
s
t
u
v
w
x
y
z

decimals

We are used to counting in hundreds, tens and units. That is the decimal way of counting. Decimals are all about tens of things and tenths of things.

The decimal point separates the whole numbers from the decimal fractions. The decimal point just marks the place. Everything before it is a whole number. Everything after it is a decimal fraction. Decimal fractions are tenths, hundredths, thousandths and so on.

	Th	H	T	U
3 is worth 3 units				3
30 is worth 3 tens			3	0
300 is worth 3 hundreds		3	0	0
3000 is worth 3 thousands	3	0	0	0

The first digit after the decimal point shows a number of tenths.
$0.3 = \frac{3}{10}$

The second digit after the decimal point shows a number of hundredths.
$0.03 = \frac{3}{100}$

The third digit after the decimal point shows thousandths.
$0.003 = \frac{3}{1000}$ and so on.

Look what happens if we start off with 0·3 and keep multiplying by 10.

	Th	H	T	U · t
				0 · 3
0·3 x 10 =				3
3 x 10 =			3	0
30 x 10 =		3	0	0
300 x 10 =	3	0	0	0

Whenever we make our number ten times bigger we move it one place to the left. We could go on and on adding more columns to the left but we don't often need numbers that big!

Look what happens if we start with 3000 and keep dividing by 10.

	Th	H	T	U · t	h	th
	3	0	0	0		
3000 ÷ 10 =		3	0	0		
300 ÷ 10 =			3	0		
30 ÷ 10 =				3		
3 ÷ 10 =				0 · 3		
0·3 ÷ 10 =				0 · 0	3	
0·03 ÷ 10 =				0 · 0	0	3

Whenever we make our number ten times smaller it moves one place to the right. We could go on and on adding columns to the right but we rarely need fractions that small!

If moving the digits like this leaves an empty space in a column we put a zero in it to keep all the other digits in the right places. (Look back and you'll see.)

Remember there is a very easy way to multiply or divide decimals by 10:

To multiply by 10 move the digits one place to the left.
To multiply by 100 move the digits two places to the left.
To multiply by 1000 move the digits three places to the left.
Write down the column headings if it helps you.

Th H T U · t h th
       4   2 · 6
       4   2   6

42·6 × 10 = 426

Th H T U · t h th
       2   1 · 7 3
    2   1   7   3

21·73 × 100 = 2173

To divide decimals by 10 we make them ten times smaller. We move the digits one place to the right.
To divide by 100 we move the digits two places to the right.
To divide by 1000 we move the digits three places to the right.

Th H T U · t h th
          1 · 2
       0 · 1 2

1·2 ÷ 10 = 0·12

Th H T U · t h th
          1 · 2
       0 · 0 1 2

1·2 ÷ 100 = 0·012

In the last example we have to put the zero in after the decimal point to show there are no tenths. It keeps the other digits in the right place.

(Of course you can multiply or divide in the ordinary way if you like but this way is quicker.)

More ...

decimals

Zeros just show that 'we haven't got any of these.'
Here are some examples:

12·0   0·4   10·6   0·03   3·20   3·02

| H | T | U·t | h |

| I | 2 ·0 | means 12 whole ones, no decimal fractions |

12·0 = 12

| 0·4 | means we have no whole numbers but we do have 4 tenths |

$0·4 = \frac{4}{10}$

| I | 0·6 | means I ten, no units, 6 tenths |

$10·6 = 10\frac{6}{10}$

| 0·0 3 | means we have no whole numbers and no tenths but we do have 3 hundredths |

$0·03 = \frac{3}{100}$

| 3·2 0 | means 3 units, 2 tenths and no hundredths. We could just write 3·2 if we liked, it would mean the same thing. |

$3·0 2 = 3\frac{2}{100}$

Here you must put the zero in to show there are no tenths. This keeps the 2 in the hundredths column.

Remember: one tenth is more than one hundredth $\frac{1}{10} = \frac{10}{100}$

0·8 is more than 0·15

$0·8 = \frac{8}{10}$ This would be $\frac{80}{100}$

$0·15 = \frac{1}{10}$ and $\frac{5}{100}$ This would be $\frac{15}{100}$

Useful decimals to learn

$0·75 = \frac{3}{4}$ $0·5 = \frac{1}{2}$ $0·25 = \frac{1}{4}$ $0·125 = \frac{1}{8}$

$0·2 = \frac{1}{5}$ $(\frac{1}{5} = \frac{2}{10})$ $0·1 = \frac{1}{10}$ $0·01 = \frac{1}{100}$

Adding and subtracting decimals
If you can add and subtract hundreds, tens and units you can add and subtract decimals.

0·5 + 0·2 = 0·7	0·6 + 0·3 = 0·9
0·6 + 0·4 = 1·0	3·5 + 1·4 = 4·9
3·5 + 1·5 = 5·0	3·5 + 1·6 = 5·1
0·5 − 0·3 = 0·2	2·5 − 1·4 = 1·1
4·5 − 1·5 = 3·0	2·0 − 0·1 = 1·9

If you need to use a written method to add or subtract decimals it helps to put the numbers underneath one another – if you do this remember to keep the decimal points under one another. That keeps all the digits lined up in the right columns. Look at these examples:

$12·5 + 9·86$

$$\begin{array}{r} 12·5 \\ +\ \ 9·86 \\ \hline 22·36 \\ 11 \end{array}$$

$24·32 + 125·01 + 3·62$

$$\begin{array}{r} 24·32 \\ +\ 125·01 \\ 3·62 \\ \hline 152·95 \\ 1 \end{array}$$

$26·25 – 3·24$

$$\begin{array}{r} 26·25 \\ -\ \ 3·24 \\ \hline 23·01 \end{array}$$

$35·14 – 2·10$

$$\begin{array}{r} 35·14 \\ -\ \ 2·10 \\ \hline 33·04 \end{array}$$

Multiplying and dividing decimals by a whole number

$0·4 \times 2 = 0·8$ $\qquad$ $1·4 \times 2 = 2·8$ $\qquad$ $0·8 \div 2 = 0·4$ $\qquad$ $2·8 \div 2 = 1·4$

If you want to do the working out in columns, remember to keep the decimal point in the right place. Look at these examples.

$$\begin{array}{r} 4·6 \\ \times\ \ 2 \\ \hline 9·2 \\ 1 \end{array}$$

$$\begin{array}{r} 52·07 \\ \times\ \ \ \ \ 5 \\ \hline 260·35 \\ 1\ \ 3 \end{array}$$

$$\begin{array}{r} 6·5 \\ 5\overline{\smash{)}32·^25} \end{array}$$

$$\begin{array}{rl} 6·5 & \\ 5\overline{\smash{)}32·5} & \\ \underline{30} & 6 \times 5 \\ 2·5 & 0·5 \times 5 \\ \underline{2·5} & \\ 0 & \text{Ans} = 6·5 \end{array}$$

Rounding decimals to the nearest whole number

15·2 is nearer to 15 than to16. If we had to round 15·2 to the nearest whole number we would round it down to 15.

15·8 is nearer to 16 than to15. If we had to round 15·8 to the nearest whole number we would round it up to16.

Giving an answer correct to a number of decimal places

Sometimes you may need to give an answer 'correct to' a number of decimal places. If you had to write 5·73 correct to one decimal place you would only have one digit after the decimal point. You would round 5·73 down to 5·7.

To write 5·78 correct to one decimal place you would round it up to 5·8. (Look up **rounding** if you want to know more about it.)

Recurring decimals

0·66666 and 0·33333 are examples of recurring decimals. The same digits are repeated over and over again; they keep recurring.

If you had to give 0·66666 correct to two decimal places you would only have two digits after the decimal point – round it up to 0·67.

To give 0·33333 correct to 2 decimal places, round it down to 0·33.

decrease

To decrease is to make something less. It is the opposite of **increase**.
If taxes are decreased people pay less money.
Decrease your speed means lessen your speed – slow down.
To decrease 20 by 5 you start with 20 and take 5 away from it.
You make it 5 less. 20 – 5 = 15

deduct

If you deduct something you take it away. If you break a window
the cost of a new one may be deducted from your pocket money.
A deduction is an amount which is taken away.

define

If you define something you explain exactly what it is.
You might define a triangle as a two-dimensional (2D) shape with
3 straight sides and 3 angles.

degrees

Some measurements in maths are made in degrees. A little circle in the
air ° stands for the word degree or degrees.
Angles are measured in degrees using a **protractor**. (This is
sometimes called an angle measurer.)
A right angle measures 90°. A whole turn in a circle measures 360°.

(Temperatures are also measured in degrees but these are on different
scales on thermometers. There is a section about the **Celsius**
thermometer in this book.)

denominator

The bottom number of a fraction is called the denominator.
It shows how many equal parts something has been split into.
$\frac{3}{5}$ The denominator of this fraction is 5.

(The top number of a fraction is called the **numerator**.)
There is more information that might be useful to you under
fractions and **common denominator**.

depth

Depth tells us how deep something is –
how far it is from the top down to the
bottom – or from the front to the back.
We might talk about the depth of
water in a swimming pool, for example,
or the depth of a shelf in a cupboard.

descend

To descend is to go down. Descending means going down.

descending order

If you need to arrange a list of numbers in descending order, the numbers will go down from the highest to the lowest. First find the highest number, then the next highest, then the next – and carry on until you get to the lowest number in the list. If you put 32 1332 5 191 16 into descending order the list would become 1332 191 32 16 5. (Always check to make sure you haven't missed one out!)

describe

If you describe something to your friends you tell them all about it. In maths you might describe the pattern in a number sequence – or a rule that helps you to work something out.

diagonal

1 When it is describing something, diagonal means sloping, or slanting.

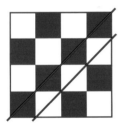

These are diagonal rows.

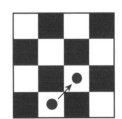

This counter has made a diagonal move. It has moved diagonally.

2 A diagonal is also the name for a straight line which joins one corner of a shape to another corner.

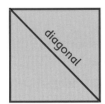 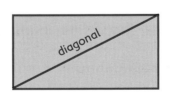 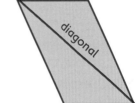

It is possible to draw five diagonals in this shape:
AC, AD, BE and BD and CE.
(Lines joining corners which are next to each other are **sides** of the shape. They are not diagonals of the shape.)

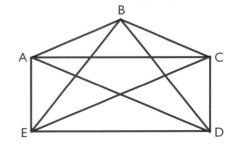

diagram

A diagram is an outline drawing.
It may be a kind of chart or a sketch-map or a simple picture – to help people understand some instructions. Sometimes it can take a lot of words to give directions or to explain something. Very often a diagram can be easier to understand. It can show information clearly without using many words at all.

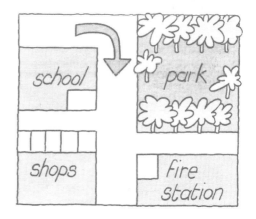

If you are stuck on a problem it is sometimes a good idea to draw a quick diagram. Mark in all the information you are given in the question. Label everything you can. It may help you to see what else you can work out and label – and what to do next.

Mandy is 5 cm taller than Petra and 5 cm shorter than Lisa.
Lisa is 1 m 48 cm tall.
How tall are the others?

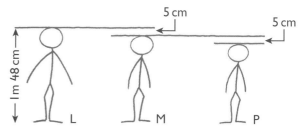

Here is Mandy (M)
5 cm taller than Petra (P)

Mandy is 5 cm shorter than Lisa (L)

Lisa is 1 m 48 cm
Mandy is 1 m 48 cm – 5 cm (1 m 43 cm)
Petra is 1 m 43 cm – 5 cm (1 m 38 cm)

Carroll diagrams and **Venn diagrams** are useful if you need to sort things into different groups.
There is a section on each of these in this book.
If you are drawing a diagram to explain something to someone else remember to make it as easy to understand as possible. Make sure you have put in everything people need to know and label things clearly.

diameter

A diameter is a straight line drawn through the centre of a **circle**.
It divides the circle into two halves.

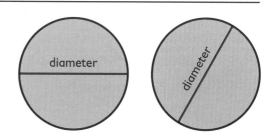

dice die

One of these can be called a die or a dice.
Two or more are **always** called dice.

Dice are usually cubes with a different number on each
face. They are used in a lot of games – and they can also
be useful in maths. When you roll a dice you can't be
sure which number will end up on top.
The section on **probability** might interest you.

difference

To find the difference between two things we have to look at them
both and compare them. We might say that one is bigger, longer or
wider than the other. In maths if we are asked to find the difference
between two things we need to find the **exact** difference between them
how much bigger, longer or wider one is than the other.

There are two ways of finding the difference between two numbers.
Here is an example of each.
Find the difference between 3 and 15.

1 We can count on from the smaller amount to the larger amount.

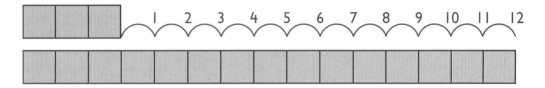

3 + 12 = 15
The difference between 3 and 15 is 12.

2 We can write down the larger amount and then take the
smaller amount away from it.

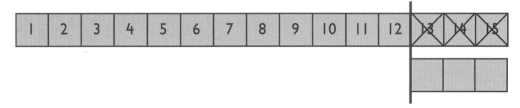

15 – 3 = 12
The difference between 3 and 15 is 12.

The second way is probably easier if you are dealing with
numbers that are a long way apart. (Remember to write
down the larger number first if you are doing it this way!)

a
b
c
Dd
e
f
g
h
i
j
k
l
m
n
o
p
q
r
s
t
u
v
w
x
y
z

a
b
c
Dd
e
f
g
h
i
j
k
l
m
n
o
p
q
r
s
t
u
v
w
x
y
z

digit

0 1 2 3 4 5 6 7 8 and 9 are digits. We use them to make up the numbers we need.

426 has 3 digits.

90 has 2 digits.

33 is a two-digit number too.

1 203 is a four-digit number.

digital clock

A digital clock is not the sort of clock that has 'hands' going round. On a digital clock or watch the numbers change to show us the time.

Look up **time** or the **twenty-four hour clock** if you want to know more about this.

dimensions

Dimensions are measurements of size. We often think of **length**, **width**, **height** and **radius**. You would need to know the dimensions of a photo before you bought a frame for it.

direction

This arrow is pointing up.

This arrow is pointing down.

This arrow is pointing left.

This arrow is pointing right.

These arrows are pointing in different directions.

'Am I going in the right direction?' means 'Am I going the right way?'

This boy is going towards the bus stop.   This one is going away from it.

If you are playing a board game you may have to move counters forwards or backwards – or sideways – or diagonally. These are all different directions.

'Turn the knob in a clockwise direction' means that the knob has to be turned round in the same direction as the hands of a clock. (If something has to go round in an anti–clockwise direction it has to go round the other way.)

You might turn round to face a different direction. A compass would show you which direction you are facing. It could be north, south, east or west – or one of the compass points in between. (Look up **compass** if you want to know more about that.)

If people are going on a journey they usually plan the route they will take before they start.
Maps are useful for finding the way. They help you to find out where you are and which direction you should be going in.
Sometimes a quick sketch–map is all that is needed.

This one shows the route from a house to the library.

Starting from the house marked with a cross, the directions would be:
– Cross the road and turn right.
– Take the second turning on your left.
– Keep going straight ahead and you will see a long building. That is the back of the library.
– Walk along the path beside it, and just around the corner you will come to the main entrance.

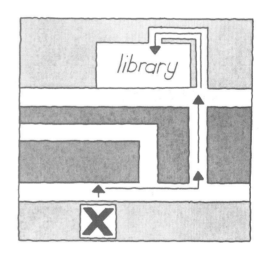

discount

A discount is an amount of money that is taken off the cost of something. Sometimes it is a fixed amount:

'£5 discount is given if this bill is paid within fourteen days.'
This means that £5 is taken off the bill if you pay it within fourteen days.
Often it is a **percentage** of the total.
10% discount means that you can take 10% of the price off the amount you pay. $10\% = \frac{10}{100} = \frac{1}{10}$

If the price is £20, the 10% discount would be $\frac{1}{10}$ of £20.

The discount would be £2. You would pay £20 – £2. You would pay £18.
(Look up **percentages** if you need to know more about that.)

a
b
c

Dd

e
f
g
h
i
j
k
l
m
n
o
p
q
r
s
t
u
v
w
x
y
z

discuss

If you discuss something, you talk about it with other people. In maths you might discuss some results you have got – or a different way of working something out.

distance

This tells us how far it is from one place to another – what the distance is between two points – how far apart they are. The shortest distance between two points is a straight line.

The international measurement of distance is based on the metre, a metric measure. (We might measure a small distance between two points in millimetres or centimetres.) In this country we sometimes measure in kilometres for longer distances but sometimes we still use miles, which is an imperial measure.

km/h stands for kilometres per hour.
mph stands for miles per hour.

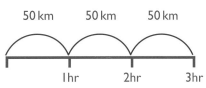

If you travel at 50 km/h we mean that you go 50 km in each hour.
If you travel for 3 hours at 50 km/h the distance you would cover would be (3 x 50) km = 150 km.

A man travels at 60 mph for 2 hr 15 min (2 $\frac{1}{4}$ hr). What distance does he travel?

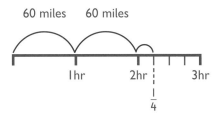

He travels 60 miles in every hour.
In 2 hours he travels (60 x 2) miles = 120 miles.

In $\frac{1}{4}$ hour he travels ($\frac{1}{4}$ of 60) miles = 15 miles.

In 2 $\frac{1}{4}$ hours he travels 135 miles.

Time (in hours) x speed (in km/h) = distance covered (in km).
Time (in hours) x speed (in mph) = distance covered (in miles).
It might help you to look up the section on **speed** as well.

distribution

When things are distributed they are passed round or spread about in some way. Leaflets are often distributed to give people information.

Weather reports tell us about the distribution of rainfall over the country: the way it is spread.
If you knew how tall everyone was in your class you could find out about the distribution of their height – how it was spread. You could find the range of their height from the shortest to the tallest and you could find out how their heights were spread in between.

divide

If you divide something in maths you split it up into equal pieces or groups.

The sign for dividing is ÷ we read it as 'divided by'.

$12 \div 4 = 3$

If you want to know more about this, look up **division**.

divisibility tests

These are quick checks to see if one number can be divided exactly by another number. They are useful if you are cancelling fractions, finding factors or dealing with problems where people or things are being sorted out into groups. (Will a number of people fit exactly into a number of coaches, for example, or will you have some spare seats?) There are simple tests for several numbers.

Here are a few worth knowing:

2s Even numbers are always exactly divisible by 2.
Even numbers end in 0, 2, 4, 6 or 8.

    396   is an even number. It can be divided exactly by 2.
           $396 \div 2 = 198$

3s Add up the digits of your number. If the answer can be divided exactly by 3, then your number can be.

    342    $3 + 4 + 2 = 9$ 9 can be divided exactly by 3.
           342 can be divided exactly by 3.
           $342 \div 3 = 114$

4s If the last two digits of a number can be divided exactly by 4, the whole number can be.

    3432   32 can be divided exactly by 4.
          3432 will divide exactly by 4.
          $3432 \div 4 = 858$

Another way is to see if half the number is an even number.

4 also divides exactly into 100 and any other number of whole hundreds.

5s 5 will divide exactly into any number ending in 5 or 0.

6s If you have an **even** number try the test for threes on it. An even number which will divide exactly by 3 can also be divided exactly by 6.

More ...

divisibility tests

a
b
c
Dd
e
f
g
h
i
j
k
l
m
n
o
p
q
r
s
t
u
v
w
x
y
z

9s Add up the digits of your number. If the answer can be divided exactly by 9 then your number can be.

432   4 + 3 + 2 = 9

432 will divide exactly by 9.

432 ÷ 9 = 48

10s If a number ends in 0 it will divide exactly by 10.

11s If you have a two-digit number where both digits are the same it will be exactly divisible by 11.
(Think of counting 11s. 11 22 33 44 55 and so on.)
If your number has three digits, add up the outside two and see if they match the middle one. If they do it will be exactly divisible by 11.
Look at these examples.

132   1 + 2 = 3   3 is in the middle.
451   4 + 1 = 5   5 is in the middle.
154   1 + 4 = 5   5 is in the middle.
880   8 + 0 = 8   8 is in the middle.

Any of these numbers could be divided exactly by 11.

division

Division is dividing into equal groups or pieces – or sharing.
The sign we use is ÷ we read it as 'divided by'.
When we multiply we collect up numbers of equal groups into one group.

When we divide we start with the whole group and split it up into smaller equal groups – or we may share it out equally between a number of other groups.

Multiplying 4 x 3 = 12   Dividing 12 ÷ 4 = 3

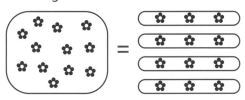

Division is the inverse of **multiplication**. (The inverse is the opposite.)
We need to divide for all the following groups.
Divide 10 people *into* 2 *equal groups.*

10 ÷ 2 = 5   There would be 5 in each group.

How many groups of three are there in 9?

9 ÷ 3 = 3   There are 3 groups of three.

Share 12 sweets *between* 3 children.

 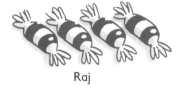 

Andy   Raj   Jason

12 ÷ 3 = 4   They could have 4 sweets each.

Group in pairs: 6 matching socks.   *Group in threes:* 15 conkers.
6 ÷ 2 = 3   There are 3 pairs.   15 ÷ 3 = 5   There are 5 groups of three.

Arrange 30 in groups of ten.
30 ÷ 10 = 3
There are 3 groups of ten.

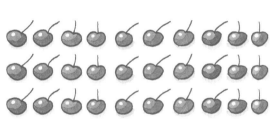

Plant 20 cabbages in rows of 4. How many rows will there be?
You could take 4 cabbages and plant them in one row.

20 − 4 = 16. There are 16 left to plant.

Plant 4 more. 16 − 4 = 12 There are 12 left to plant.

Plant 4 more. 12 − 4 = 8   There are 8 left to plant.

Plant 4 more. 8 − 4 = 4   There are 4 still to plant.

Plant 4 more. 4 − 4 = 0   They are all planted.

There are 5 rows of cabbages.

This kind of dividing is called **repeated subtraction**.

More ...

a
b
c
Dd
e
f
g
h
i
j
k
l
m
n
o
p
q
r
s
t
u
v
w
x
y
z

Another way of doing this would be to divide the 20 cabbages into groups of 4. (One group for each row.)

20 ÷ 4 = 5

There would be 5 rows of cabbages.

Division can be written down like this:

12 ÷ 4 = 3   or $\frac{3}{4\overline{)12}}$ or $4\underline{\lfloor 12}$ or $\frac{12}{4} = 3$

We could say *12 divided by 4 equals ....?*
or *How many fours are there in 12?*

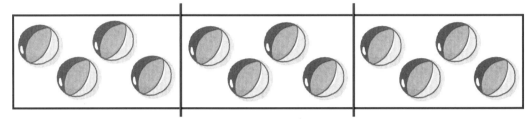

Sometimes things won't divide exactly.
If you share 7 pencils between 3 people,
they can have 2 each and there will be
one left over.

Anything that is left over at the end
is called the **remainder**.
7 ÷ 3 = 2 remainder 1
We can write 2 rem 1 or 2 r 1 to
save time.

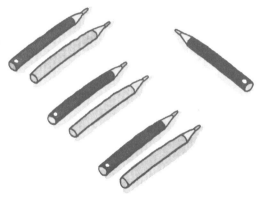

When we have divided something the answer is called the **quotient**.
(Say 'kwo-shnt'.) (Look this up if you need to know more about it.)

We divide to find parts of something:

To find half of something ($\frac{1}{2}$) divide it by 2.

To find a third of something ($\frac{1}{3}$) divide it by 3.

To find a quarter of something ($\frac{1}{4}$) divide it by 4.

To find a fifth of something ($\frac{1}{5}$) divide it by 5, and so on.

We may divide numbers of things:
When we are dividing numbers of things we can often use
the multiplication tables to help us. They show us how many
groups of a certain size we can make out of a larger number.

We know that 3 x 6 = 18 so we can say:
How many lots of 6 are there in 18? 3

How many lots of 3 are there in 18? 6

We could also quickly find:
How many groups of 6 can we make out of 18?
How many groups of 3 can we make out of 18?
How many 6s make 18?
How many 3s are there in 18?

Written methods of division
Sometimes you may have bigger numbers that are not so easy to work out. It's useful to know a method of writing it all down so that you can work out a bit at a time. These examples won't teach you how to divide bigger numbers – but they might help you to remember about it if you have forgotten. Ask for help if you need it.

Look at this way of working out 148 ÷ 6.
We need to know how many lots of 6 there are in 148.
It helps to make an estimate first:
We know that 10 lots of 6 = 60. So 20 lots of 6 = 120.
We can take that from 148. (30 lots of 6 = 180. That's too much.)

```
6 ⌐148
  −120   That's 20 lots of 6.   (If we take that away from 148 we have 28 left.)
    28                          (4 lots of 6 = 24. We can get 4 lots of 6 out of 28)
  − 24   That's 4 lots of 6.    (If we take that away from 28 we only have 4 left)
     4
```

The 4 at the end is left over. It's the remainder.
The answer is 24 r4.

More …

a
b
c

Dd

e
f
g
h
i
j
k
l
m
n
o
p
q
r
s
t
u
v
w
x
y
z

You can use the same method when you are dealing with larger numbers. Look at this example: 4596 ÷ 21.

We know that 2100 is 100 lots of 21, so 200 lots of 21 = 4200, so the answer will be greater than 200.

```
21⟌4596
   − 4200        200 x 21
      396
     − 210        10 x 21
       186
      − 168        8 x 21
        18        Answer = 218 r18
```

> Always remember to keep your columns of figures straight so they don't get muddled up with each other.

You may have been using a different method – like this one. This way we have to work out part of the multiplication table first. If we needed to divide 82 by 21 we would work out:

```
       3r 19          2 x 21 = 42
21⟌82               3 x 21 = 63
   − 63               4 x 21 = 84
     19       Answer = 3 r19
```

In the next example we have an extra bit to deal with. We work out the first bit in the same way then we bring the 3 down beside the 4 so there is more space for the working out.

```
        12r 1         2 x 21 = 42
21⟌253              3 x 21 = 63
   − 21↓
      43
    − 42
       1        Answer = 12 r1
```

The next example goes one step further.

```
        218r 18     2 x 21 = 42
21⟌4596            3 x 21 = 63
   − 42↓↓
      39|            9 x 21 = 189
    − 21↓            8 x 21 = 168
      186
      168
       18        Answer = 218 r18
```

(We know that 1 x 21 = 21 and 10 x 21 = 210 so we can work out the bit of the table we think we might need. We don't have to work out the whole table.)

dodecagon

A dodecagon is a 2D shape with 12 straight sides and 12 angles. If all of the sides and all of the angles are equal it is called a **regular** dodecagon.

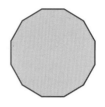

regular dodecagon

dodecahedron *(The plural is dodecahedra)*

This is a 3D shape with 12 faces. If all the faces are exactly the same size and shape it is called a regular dodecahedron and each face will be a regular pentagon. (A pentagon is a 2D five-sided shape.)

double

If you double something you make it twice as big – or twice as much. You multiply it by 2.

If you have £5 and you double your money you end up with £10 (£5 + another £5 or £5 x 2).

Doubling is the same as multiplying by 2.
8 + 8 = 16   8 x 2 = 16

The opposite of doubling is halving. (That is the same as dividing by 2).

doubles

5 + 5 = 10   5 x 2 = 10   5 doubled = 10

Two numbers that are both the same are sometimes called doubles.
31 + 31 are doubles.   120 + 120 are doubles.

If you practise adding doubles you'll find you get quicker at it.

Near doubles are numbers that are very nearly doubles.
14 + 13 are near doubles.
14 + 14 = 28 so 14 + 13 is one less.
14 + 13 = 27

If you can add 15 + 15 quickly 15 + 16 is easy too.
If 15 + 15 = 30   15 + 16 = 30 + 1 more.
15 + 16 = 31.

a
b
c
d
Ee
f
g
h
i
j
k
l
m
n
o
p
q
r
s
t
u
v
w
x
y
z

enough

(Say 'eenuff'.) If you had 6 chairs for 6 people you would have enough chairs for them all. (If you had more than 6 chairs for them you would have more than enough!) If you had less than 6 chairs for 6 people you would have less than you needed – you would have too few. You wouldn't have enough.

equation

Equations are sometimes called maths sentences or number sentences. They always follow the same pattern. Whatever comes before the equals sign (**=**) is worth the same as whatever comes after it. The two sides are equal.

13 apples + 2 apples = 15 apples.

$10 = 6 + 4$ $\qquad$ $6 \times 1 = 3 \times 2$

$14 \div 2 = 7$ $\qquad$ $17 - 3 = 18 - 4$

$1\frac{1}{2} = \frac{1}{2} + \frac{1}{2} + \frac{1}{2}$

These are all equations.

Sometimes there is a missing number and you have to find out what it is. (There may be an empty box or a letter in the place where it should be.)

$8 + \square = 10$ $\quad$ $8 + 2 = 10$ $\qquad\qquad$ $\square - 4 = 2$ $\quad$ $6 - 4 = 2$

$x + 5 = 8$
$3 + 5 = 8$
$x = 3$

Sometimes more than one number is missing. Look at this example.

$\triangle + \square = 10$

There are lots of possible answers for this. You could use any two numbers that make up 10.

Equations with missing numbers are just like puzzles. Here is another way of solving them.

Remember: equations are like balancing scales. The amount on one side equals the amount on the other side.

If you add something to one side you must add the same amount to the other side to keep them balancing.

If you take something away from one side you must take the same amount from the other side to keep them balanced.

It is the same with multiplying or dividing. Whatever you do to one side you must do to the other side. Then both sides will stay equal.

Look at this example.
(You might be asked to *Find* x or *Find the value of* x or
Solve the equation.)
$x + 3 = 27$

Take 3 away from each side and you will be left with the
answer you need.
$x = 24$

Check the answer to see if it's right. Go back to the beginning:
$x + 3 = 27$.
Put 24 in the place of x and you get $24 + 3 = 27$.

---

equilateral triangle

Equilateral means having equal sides.
Equi- comes from a Latin word that
means equal, **lateral** comes from a
word that means side.
All 3 sides of an equilateral triangle
are equal in length.
The angles are all equal too.
They each measure 60°.

An equilateral triangle has 3 lines of symmetry.

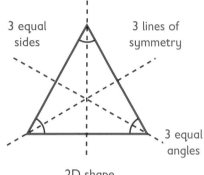

3 equal sides

3 lines of symmetry

3 equal angles

2D shape

---

equivalent

Equivalent means of equal value: **equi-val-ent**. Things which
are equivalent to each other are worth the same. We use
the equals sign to show this:

6 + 6 is equivalent to 12 $6 + 6 = 12$
6 x 2 is equivalent to 3 x 4 $6 \times 2 = 3 \times 4$

A £1 coin is equivalent to 10 ten pence pieces.
It is worth the same amount of money. It has the same value.
£1 = 10 x 10p.

$\frac{1}{2}$ litre + $\frac{1}{2}$ litre is equivalent to 1 litre.

$\frac{1}{2}$ litre + $\frac{1}{2}$ litre = 1 litre

These are equivalent fractions:

$\frac{1}{2} = \frac{2}{4} = \frac{3}{6} = \frac{4}{8} = \frac{5}{10}$

Fractions, decimals and percentages can be equivalent to
each other too.

$50\% = \frac{50}{100} = \frac{5}{10} = \frac{1}{2}$ $0\cdot5 = \frac{5}{10} = \frac{1}{2}$

a
b
c
d
Ee
f
g
h
i
j
k
l
m
n
o
p
q
r
s
t
u
v
w
x
y
z

a
b
c
d
Ee
f
g
h
i
j
k
l
m
n
o
p
q
r
s
t
u
v
w
x
y
z

estimate

An estimate is a sensible guess. If you have to estimate the number of beans in a jar you look carefully at the beans and at the size of the jar before you guess how many there are.

It is useful to base an estimate on something you know. If you know your own height, for example, it is easier to estimate someone else's.

If you have to work out something like 38 + 49 you might estimate the answer first. It looks a bit less than 40 + 50. A bit less than 90. If your answer is not close to your estimate you can check to see where you've gone wrong. You may find it useful to look up **rounding** (about 'rounding' numbers up or down) or **approximation**.

---

even numbers

Even numbers are whole numbers that can be divided exactly by 2. Nothing is left over.

$6 \div 2 = 3$ 6 is an even number.
$7 \div 2 = 3$ and 1 is left over.
7 is **not** an even number. (See the odd one?)

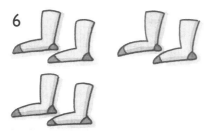 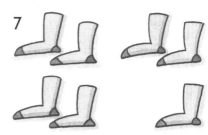

$8 \div 2 = 4$ 8 is an even number.
$9 \div 2 = 4$ and 1 is left over.
9 is **not** an even number.

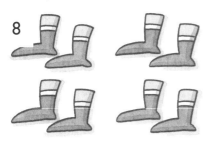 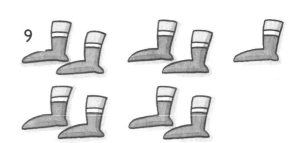

All numbers that end in 2, 4, 6, 8 or 0 are even numbers.
These are all even numbers: 134 778 1276 5000

Numbers that are **not** even are called **odd numbers**.

exchange

If you buy something that's the wrong size you might exchange it for a different one. If you exchange something you give it to someone and get something else in return.

Someone might exchange a 20p coin for two 10p coins. If you are working in a group you might exchange ideas about the work you are doing.

If you have been doing different work you might tell each other what you have found out. You would exchange information.

expensive

If something is expensive it costs a lot. It is dear.
(The opposite is cheap.)

explain

If you explain something to people you tell them about it in a way that they can understand.

If you have been working something out you might explain how you got your answer.

If you are asked to explain your method of doing something you have to explain the way you did it – how you worked it out or how you went about it.

If you are asked to explain your reasoning you have to explain how you thought it through; how you worked it out.

exterior

Exterior means outside. The exterior angles of a triangle are outside the triangle. An exterior angle can be formed by making one of the sides of the triangle longer so that it sticks out. (The opposite is **interior**, meaning inside.)
a, **b**, and **c** are all exterior angles of the triangle.

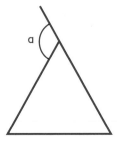
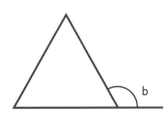

a
b
c
d
e
Ff
g
h
i
j
k
l
m
n
o
p
q
r
s
t
u
v
w
x
y
z

factor

A factor is a whole number which will divide exactly into another whole number.

3 is a factor of 12 ($12 \div 3 = 4$)

4 is a factor of 12 ($12 \div 4 = 3$)

2 and 6 are factors of 12 as well.

$12 \div 2 = 6$ $12 \div 6 = 2$

Numbers which are multiplied together are factors of the answer.

$2 \times 4 = 8$

2 is a factor of 8   4 is a factor of 8.

Common factor

When we want to cancel or order fractions we sometimes need to find a common factor.

This is a number that will divide exactly into both the top and the bottom of the fraction.

Look at $\frac{12}{15}$

2 will divide exactly into 12 but not into 15

3 will divide exactly into both 12 and 15

3 is a common factor of 12 and 15.

$\frac{\cancel{12}^{4}}{\cancel{15}_{5}} = \frac{4}{5}$

Prime factor

A prime factor is a factor which is also a prime number. (Remember, a prime number can only be divided exactly by itself and 1. It can't be broken down into smaller equal groups.)

3 is a prime factor of 12

4 is also a factor of 12 but it isn't a prime factor because you can break 4 down into 2×2.

The prime factors of 12 are 2, 2 and 3:

$2 \times 2 \times 3 = 12$

---

factorize

Read the section about **factors** first if you are not sure about them. (It is just before this one.)

If you factorize a number you break it down into its factors.

$18 = 2 \times 9 = 2 \times 3 \times 3$

The prime factors of 18 are 2, 3 and 3.

$30 = 2 \times 15 = 2 \times 3 \times 5$

The prime factors of 30 are 2, 3 and 5.

Fahrenheit

(Say 'Farrenhite'.) Fahrenheit is the name of a kind of thermometer and its measuring scale.

The freezing point of water is marked as 32 degrees Fahrenheit (32°F). The boiling point of water is marked as 212 degrees Fahrenheit (212°F). Nowadays the **Celsius** (or centigrade) scale is used more often. On the Celsius scale, the freezing point of water is marked as 0 degrees Celsius (0°C), and the boiling point as 100 degrees Celsius (100°C). The diagram below shows a way to compare the two scales.

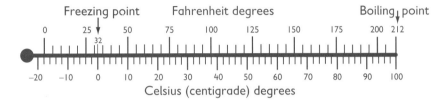

first

The first number in a list is the one that comes right at the beginning. The first letter of the alphabet is A. The second letter is B, the third is C and so on.

The person who wins a race comes first (1st). The next person to finish comes second (2nd), the next comes third (3rd). The last one comes right at the end.

Words like first, second and third are called **ordinal numbers**. They tell us the order that things or people come in or their place in a list. See page 188 if you want to know about more of these numbers.

foot feet

A foot is a measure of length in the imperial system.

12 inches (in)	= 1 foot
3 feet (ft)	= 1 yard
1760 yards (yd)	= 1 mile.

1 foot measures about 30 cm.

formula   *(The plural is formulae)*

(Say 'form–you–lee'.) In maths a formula is a quick way of writing down a rule.
The formula for finding the area of a rectangle is   **a = l x b**.
a stands for the area of the rectangle.
l stands for the length of the rectangle.
b stands for the breadth (width) of the rectangle.
A formula gives us a pattern for working something out.
(Find more examples of formulae under **distance** and **speed**.)

fractions

Fractions are parts of something. The bottom number of a fraction is called the de**nom**inator. It is the **name** of the fraction and tells us the number of equal parts something has been divided into.

The top **number** of a fraction is called the **num**erator. It tells us how many of those parts we are dealing with.

numerator
_____
denominator

$\frac{1}{2}$ is called a half. It means that something has been divided into 2 equal parts or groups.

We have one piece out of the two. $\frac{1}{2}$

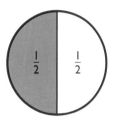

$\frac{1}{2}$ is shaded. $\frac{1}{2}$ is unshaded.

$\frac{2}{3}$ is called two thirds. It means that something has been divided into 3 equal parts or groups and we have 2 of them.

We have 2 pieces out of the three. $\frac{2}{3}$

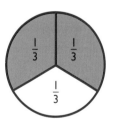

$\frac{2}{3}$ is shaded. $\frac{1}{3}$ is unshaded.

$\frac{3}{4}$ is called three quarters. Something has been divided into 4 equal parts or groups and we have 3 of them.

We have 3 pieces out of the four. $\frac{3}{4}$

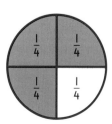

$\frac{3}{4}$ is shaded. $\frac{1}{4}$ is unshaded.

If we need to find $\frac{1}{2}$ of something we divide it by 2.

If we need to find $\frac{1}{3}$ of something we divide it by 3.

If we need to find $\frac{1}{4}$ of something we divide it by 4.

If we need to find $\frac{1}{5}$ of something we divide it by 5 and so on.

To find $\frac{2}{3}$ of something, find $\frac{1}{3}$ of it then multiply by 2.

To find $\frac{5}{6}$ of something, find $\frac{1}{6}$ of it then multiply by 5.

To find $\frac{9}{10}$ of something, find $\frac{1}{10}$ of it then multiply by 9.

Whole numbers

Two halves make one whole.
Three thirds make one whole.
Four quarters make one whole.

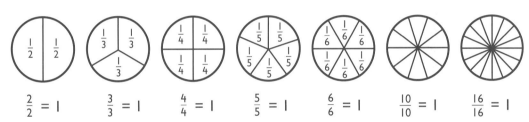

$$\frac{2}{2} = 1 \qquad \frac{3}{3} = 1 \qquad \frac{4}{4} = 1 \qquad \frac{5}{5} = 1 \qquad \frac{6}{6} = 1 \qquad \frac{10}{10} = 1 \qquad \frac{16}{16} = 1$$

If the numerator and the denominator are the same, the fraction is equal to 1 whole one. Something has been divided up into a number of pieces and we have all of them.

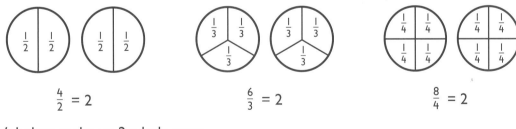

$$\frac{4}{2} = 2 \qquad\qquad \frac{6}{3} = 2 \qquad\qquad \frac{8}{4} = 2$$

4 halves make up 2 whole ones.
6 thirds make up 2 whole ones.
8 quarters make up 2 whole ones.

Mixed numbers

A mixed number has both whole numbers and fractions.
These are all mixed numbers.

$$2\frac{1}{2} \quad 1\frac{7}{8} \quad 12\frac{5}{6} \quad 15\frac{2}{7}$$

More ...

Proper fractions

In a proper fraction the numerator is less than the denominator.

Improper fractions

These are sometimes called top-heavy fractions.
The numerator is more than the denominator.

$$\frac{5}{4} \qquad \frac{10}{6} \qquad \frac{12}{6} \qquad \frac{10}{3}$$

These are all improper fractions.
Improper fractions can be changed to **whole numbers** or **mixed numbers**.

$\frac{4}{4} = 1$ so $\frac{5}{4} = 1\frac{1}{4}$

   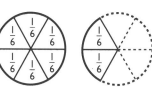

$\frac{6}{6} = 1$ so $\frac{7}{6} = 1\frac{1}{6}$ and $\frac{8}{6} = 1\frac{2}{6}$

To change an improper fraction to whole or mixed numbers we divide the numerator by the denominator. That will tell us how many whole numbers we can make. If there are any remainders they will be the fractions that are left over.

$$\frac{10}{6} = 1\frac{4}{6} \qquad \frac{12}{6} = 2 \qquad \frac{13}{6} = 2\frac{1}{6}$$

$$\frac{27}{5} = 5\frac{2}{5} \qquad \frac{28}{5} = 5\frac{3}{5} \qquad \frac{23}{10} = 2\frac{3}{10}$$

To change mixed numbers to improper fractions

Remember: $1 = \frac{2}{2} = \frac{3}{3} = \frac{4}{4} = \frac{5}{5}$ and so on.

1 Look to see the kind of fraction you have.
2 Change your whole numbers to this kind of fraction. It may help you to think of them as whole cakes to be cut into equal pieces.
3 Add on the fraction you have and show how many pieces you have altogether.

$2\frac{7}{8} =$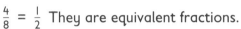

$2\frac{7}{8} = \frac{8}{8} + \frac{8}{8} + \frac{7}{8} = \frac{23}{8}$

$3\frac{1}{3} =$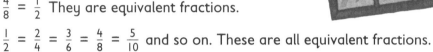

I whole one = 3 thirds = $\frac{3}{3}$

3 whole ones = 3 x 3 thirds = $\frac{9}{3}$

$3\frac{1}{3}$ = 10 thirds = $\frac{10}{3}$

Equivalent fractions

These are fractions of equal value. They are worth the same.

If you eat $\frac{4}{8}$ of a bar of chocolate you have eaten four pieces out of the eight. You have eaten half of it.

$\frac{4}{8} = \frac{1}{2}$ They are equivalent fractions.

$\frac{1}{2} = \frac{2}{4} = \frac{3}{6} = \frac{4}{8} = \frac{5}{10}$ and so on. These are all equivalent fractions.

Here are some more examples of equivalent fractions:

$\frac{1}{3} = \frac{2}{6} = \frac{3}{9} = \frac{4}{12} = \frac{5}{15}$ and so on. $\frac{1}{10} = \frac{2}{20} = \frac{3}{30} = \frac{4}{40}$ and so on.

To change a fraction to an equivalent fraction

If we multiply anything by 1 we don't change its value.
3 x 1 = 3   £5 x 1 = £5

If we multiply the numerator and the denominator of a fraction by the same number we don't change its value. It is the same as multiplying by $\frac{2}{2}$ or $\frac{3}{3}$ or $\frac{4}{4}$ and so on.

$\frac{1}{2} = \frac{1 \times 4}{2 \times 4} = \frac{4}{8}$ $\frac{1}{2} \times \frac{4}{4} = \frac{4}{8}$ $\frac{1}{2} = \frac{4}{8}$

$\frac{3}{5} = \frac{3 \times 2}{5 \times 2} = \frac{6}{10}$ $\frac{3}{5} \times \frac{2}{2} = \frac{6}{10}$ $\frac{3}{5} = \frac{6}{10}$

If you multiply the top number of a fraction by something you must multiply the bottom number by the same thing to keep it equivalent.

$\frac{4}{6} = \frac{12}{\square}$ (4 x 3 = 12
6 x 3 = 18)

$\frac{4}{6} = \frac{12}{18}$

The same thing happens if we divide by 1.
If we divide a fraction by $\frac{2}{2}$ or $\frac{3}{3}$ or $\frac{4}{4}$ and so on, we don't change its value.

If you divide the top number of a fraction by something you must divide the bottom number by the same thing to keep it equivalent.

$\frac{15}{25} = \frac{3}{\square}$ (15 ÷ 5 = 3
25 ÷ 5 = 5)

$\frac{15}{25} = \frac{3}{5}$

a
b
c
d
e
Ff
g
h
i
j
k
l
m
n
o
p
q
r
s
t
u
v
w
x
y
z

More ...

fractions

a
b
c
d
e
Ff
g
h
i
j
k
l
m
n
o
p
q
r
s
t
u
v
w
x
y
z

Cancelling

We use cancelling when we divide the numerator and denominator of a fraction by the same number.

$$\frac{4}{16} = \frac{\cancel{4} \times 1}{\cancel{4} \times 4} = \frac{1}{4} \quad \text{or} \quad \frac{\cancel{4}^{1}}{\cancel{16}_{4}} = \frac{1}{4}$$

$$\frac{2}{8} = \frac{\cancel{2} \times 1}{\cancel{2} \times 4} = \frac{1}{4} \quad \text{or} \quad \frac{\cancel{2}^{1}}{\cancel{8}_{4}} = \frac{1}{4}$$

A number that will divide exactly into both the numerator and the denominator is a common factor. If you can find a common factor you can cancel to simplify a fraction, or reduce it to its lowest terms. Look up **factor** if you want to know more about this.

Reduce to its lowest terms (simplify)

To simplify a fraction or bring it to its lowest terms we bring the fraction down to the smallest, easiest numbers we can. We cancel as much as possible. We change improper fractions to whole or mixed numbers.

$$\frac{\cancel{18}^{6}}{\cancel{3}_{1}} = \frac{6}{1} = 6 \qquad \frac{10}{9} = 1\frac{1}{9} \qquad \frac{\cancel{14}^{7}}{\cancel{16}_{8}} = \frac{7}{8}$$

$$\frac{12}{10} = 1\frac{\cancel{2}^{1}}{\cancel{10}_{5}} = 1\frac{1}{5} \qquad \frac{\cancel{20}^{1}}{\cancel{100}_{5}} = \frac{1}{5}$$

Adding and subtracting fractions

It is easy to add and subtract fractions if they have the same denominator.

3 fifths + 1 fifth = 4 fifths

$$\frac{3}{5} + \frac{1}{5} = \frac{4}{5}$$

5 sixths − 4 sixths = 1 sixth

$$\frac{5}{6} - \frac{4}{6} = \frac{1}{6}$$

If we are dealing with different kinds of fractions we have to change them to the same sort before we can add or subtract them. We need to find a **common denominator**.

For $\frac{2}{5} + \frac{3}{10}$ 10 could be the common denominator.

5 will divide into 10 exactly.
10 will divide into 10 exactly.
Both fractions could be tenths.

$$\frac{2}{5} = \frac{\square}{10} \qquad \begin{array}{l} 2 \times 2 = 4 \\ 5 \times 2 = 10 \end{array} \qquad \frac{2}{5} = \frac{4}{10}$$

$\frac{3}{10}$ does not need to be changed.

$$\frac{2}{5} + \frac{3}{10} = \frac{4}{10} + \frac{3}{10} = \frac{7}{10}$$

For $\frac{2}{3}$ and $\frac{1}{2}$, 6 could be the common denominator.

3 will divide into 6 exactly.
2 will divide into 6 exactly.
Both fractions could be sixths.

$$3\frac{2}{3} - 1\frac{1}{2}$$

$$= 2\frac{2}{3} - \frac{1}{2}$$

$$= 2\frac{4}{6} - \frac{3}{6}$$

$$= 2\frac{1}{6}$$

Fractions and decimals
When people talk about fractions they usually mean the
sort with a numerator and a denominator.
Decimal fractions are usually just called decimals. There is a
separate section under **decimals** about them.
Look up **order** if you want to see examples of putting
fractions and decimals into order.

frequency

People at a railway station often ask about the frequency of
trains. They want to know how frequently they run – how
often they run. It might be a number of times an hour for
example – or a number of times a day.
The frequency of something can tell us how often it happens
– or occurs – or how common it is.
Look at this frequency table. It is about the kinds of ice
cream chosen at a party.

Choice of ice cream	
chocolate	4
vanilla	2
strawberry	6
raspberry	3
butterscotch	2
coffee	1

Strawberry ice cream was the most common choice – it was
chosen most often.
Coffee ice cream was the least common choice – only one
person chose it.

a
b
c
d
e
f
Gg
h
i
j
k
l
m
n
o
p
q
r
s
t
u
v
w
x
y
z

gram

A gram is a metric measure of mass (or weight).

1000 milligrams (mg)	=	1 gram (g)
1000 grams	=	1 kilogram (kg)
1000 kilograms	=	1 tonne

In the imperial system of weighing, 28 grams are about 1 ounce (oz).
1 kilogram is about 2·2 pounds (lbs).
(These pounds are a measurement of weight. They don't have anything to do with money.)

graphs

A graph is a special kind of chart or diagram. It shows information clearly without using a lot of words or lists of numbers.
One way of doing this is to use a **pictogram**. The first example shows the numbers of badges that some children have collected.

Pictogram
This can be called a **picture graph**, a **pictograph** or **pictogram**. Most people seem to call it a pictogram. The information is shown by a series of little pictures or symbols.

Badges collected

Andy ⭐⭐⭐⭐   ⭐

Niall ⭐⭐⭐   represents (stands for) 1 badge

Ashley ⭐⭐⭐

Gita ⭐⭐⭐⭐⭐

Jenny ⭐⭐

Viv ⭐⭐⭐

The pictogram above could have been drawn like this:

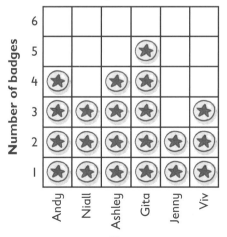

Badges collected

⭐ represents (stands for) 1 badge

If you are drawing a pictogram give it a title that tells people what it's about.

Choose a very simple little picture or symbol because you may need to copy a lot of them.

Always say what one symbol stands for.

Make sure your symbols are above one another and in tidy rows so that people can see your information easily.

If you are dealing with large numbers you can make one symbol stand for more than one.

Look at the next example: one symbol stands for 10 people.

40 people had arranged an outing to York, 30 were going to Hampton Court, 60 were going to London and 25 were going to Bournemouth.

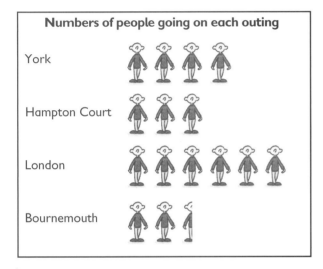

 represents (stands for) 10 people.

We wrote the place names down first before we started drawing otherwise it would have been hard to get the symbols above each other.

 stood for 10 people

 stood for 20 people

We needed to show 25 for Bournemouth. 5 is half of 10 so we had to draw half a symbol to stand for 5.

 stood for 25.

More ...

a
b
c
d
e
f
Gg
h
i
j
k
l
m
n
o
p
q
r
s
t
u
v
w
x
y
z

Bar charts

A bar chart is a kind of graph where the information is shown in bars. The bars can be vertical (straight up) or horizontal (straight across.) Sometimes bar charts are called bar graphs or column graphs. There is an example here. Look up **bar chart** if you need to know a bit more about them.

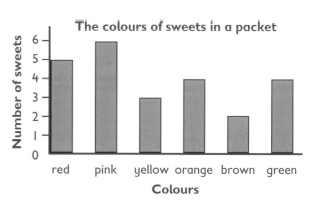

The colours of sweets in a packet

Bar line charts

A bar line chart is very much like a bar chart, but lines are used to show the information instead of the wider bars. (They are sometimes called bar line graphs or stick graphs.) This example uses the same information as the bar chart, so you can compare them.

The colours of sweets in a packet

Line graphs

Sometimes only the points that would be at the tops of lines are marked in or 'plotted' and then the points are joined together. This is called a line graph.

When the points in this graph are joined together they make a straight line. Sometimes the lines go up and down and sometimes they can be curved.

The one shown here is also a conversion graph. You can easily see that 1 kilogram of these apples costs £1.20 and 2 kilograms cost £2.40.

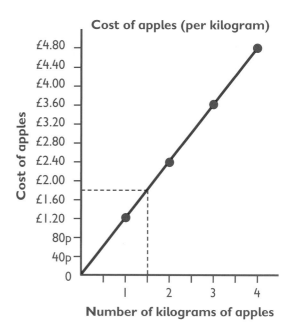

Cost of apples (per kilogram)

$1\frac{1}{2}$ kilograms of apples would cost half-way between those two amounts.

We can read off in-between amounts on this sort of graph. It can save a lot of time.

It doesn't **always** make sense to join up points or the tops of lines like this though. Look at the bar line chart about sweets again. The spaces in between the lines don't mean anything. There were 5 red sweets and there were 6 pink ones and so on. They are all quite separate.

Drawing a graph

It is easiest to work on squared paper or special graph paper when you are drawing a graph. Your paper may not be big enough for you to use one square for each thing you are counting. You may have to let each square stand for two – or more. (This is called using a smaller scale.)

Remember:

1 Use a sharp pencil.

2 Put a heading or title in to tell people what your graph is about.

3 Fit your graph onto your page so that it is as easy to see and understand as possible. (Leave enough space to draw both axes.)

4 Label the axes so that people can understand your information.

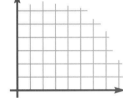

Look out for words with **graph** in them – see if they have something to do with writing or drawing!

Greenwich Mean Time (GMT)

(Say 'Grenidge' Mean Time.) The world rotates through 360° every day. It takes 24 hours for it to make a whole turn, so in one hour it turns through 15°. (360 ÷ 24 = 15)
A whole day lasts for 24 hours. When it is day-time in this country it is night-time on the other side of the world.

If you travel to another country you may have to change the time on your watch. If you are going to phone someone who lives in another country you may need to check what time it is there – if they are a long way away it could be the middle of the night!

When it is 12 noon (midday) in London it is only 7am in New York. They are 5 hours behind London. In Delhi it would be 5pm though – they are 5 hours ahead of London.

The time is measured to the east and to the west from Greenwich in London and it is called Greenwich Mean Time.

a
b
c
d
e
f
Gg
h
i
j
k
l
m
n
o
p
q
r
s
t
u
v
w
x
y
z

a
b
c
d
e
f
Gg
h
i
j
k
l
m
n
o
p
q
r
s
t
u
v
w
x
y
z

grid

A grid is a framework of lines. Grids can be used in a lot of different ways. A table of information is often arranged in a grid. It keeps everything in straight rows and columns, which makes it easy for you to look things up.

The lines of a grid are often drawn across each other in a criss-cross pattern, making a network of squares. You can draw on the lines of a grid like this – they can help you to draw shapes, diagrams, or plans.

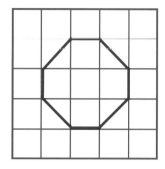

The squares on this kind of grid can be very useful too. A number grid can be used for making counting patterns, for example.

1	2	3	4	5	6	7	8	9	10
11	12	13	14	15	16	17	18	19	20
21	22	23	24	25	26	27	28	29	30
31	32	33	34	35	36	37	38	39	40
41	42	43	44	45	46	47	48	49	50
51	52	53	54	55	56	57	58	59	60
61	62	63	64	65	66	67	68	69	70
71	72	73	74	75	76	77	78	79	80
81	82	83	84	85	86	87	88	89	90
91	92	93	94	95	96	97	98	99	100

Sometimes the lines at the edge of a grid have numbers or letters on them. This helps people to find a certain square. You can often see grids like that on maps. They make it easier to find the place you are looking for. Here the square C1 shows you where the school is.

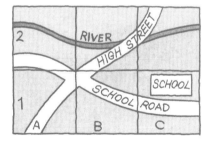

guess

(Say 'gess'.) If you guess something, you don't work it all out – you just say what you think it might be. For example you might guess how many marbles there are in a bag.

If you counted the marbles later you would see how near you were to the right number. If your guess was too low, it was not enough. If your guess was too high, it was too much.

If your guess was the same as the real answer – or if it was only just under it or just over it, then it was a good guess!

Sometimes you need to think more carefully before you make a guess. Look up **estimate** or **approximation** if you want to know more about that.

half *(The plural is halves)*

(Say 'harf' and 'harves'.) If something is divided into two equal parts or groups, each part is called a half.

It can be written as $\frac{1}{2}$ (One part out of the two.)

Two halves make up a whole one.

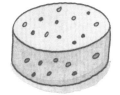 

$$\frac{1}{2} + \frac{1}{2} = 1 \qquad\qquad \frac{2}{2} = 1$$

$$\frac{1}{2}\,kg + \frac{1}{2}\,kg = 1\,kg \qquad 2 \times \frac{1}{2}\,kg = 1\,kg$$

To find half of something we divide it by 2. We halve it.

Half of 10 is 5. $10 \div 2 = 5$

halve

(Say 'harve'.) To halve something we divide it into two equal parts. Each part is called a half.
If we need to halve a number or an amount of something we divide it by 2.

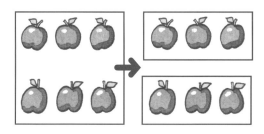   

(The opposite of halving is doubling.)

height

(Say 'hite'.) The height of something tells you how far it is from the bottom to the top. It tells you how high it is. Your height is the measurement from the bottom of your feet to the top of your head. It tells you how tall you are.

hemisphere

Hemi comes from a Greek word that means half.
A hemi-sphere is the shape of half a sphere.
It has one flat surface and the rest of it is curved.

heptagon

A heptagon is a 2D shape which has 7 sides and 7 angles. If all the sides and angles are equal it is called a regular heptagon.

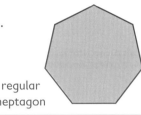

regular
heptagon

heptagonal

Heptagonal means shaped like a heptagon: with 7 angles and 7 sides.

hexagon

A hexagon is a 2D shape which has 6 sides and 6 angles. If all the sides and angles are equal it is called a regular hexagon.

regular   irregular

hexagonal

Hexagonal means shaped like a hexagon: having six sides and six angles.

hollow

This chocolate egg is hollow: look – when it is broken open there's a space in the middle.

If a cube or a sphere is hollow it has a space inside it. You might carry something very small in a hollow in your hand – you could curve your hand and make a little space for it. A hollow is a space inside something.

horizontal

Horizontal means level, parallel to the horizon.
If you have a glass of water and tilt it, the surface of the water stays level. It is still horizontal.

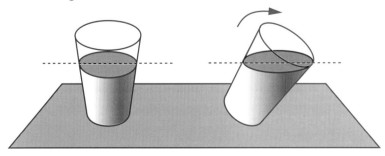

A table top should be a horizontal surface – level and flat.

If you are writing on a lined page the lines are horizontal.
If the book has squared pages it will have vertical lines going from top to bottom as well.

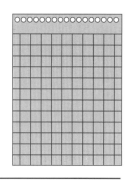

hour

> 60 seconds = 1 minute (min)
> 60 minutes = 1 hour (hr)
> 24 hours   = 1 day

To change hours into minutes multiply the hours by 60.
To change minutes into hours divide the minutes by 60.
There is more information about hours under **time**, the **twenty-four hour clock** and **timetable**.

hundreds boundary

7 + 5 = 12. It is 7 + 3 and 2 more. The number has crossed a tens boundary. It has gone over a multiple of 10.

27 + 5 = 32. It is 27 + 3 and 2 more. It has also crossed a tens boundary, 30.

60 + 48 = 108. It is 60 + 40 (making 100) and 8 more. The number has crossed a hundreds boundary.

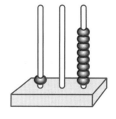

```
H T U
  6 0
+ 4 8
─────
1 0 8
```

hundredth

1 When 99 people have finished running a marathon, the next person to finish is the hundredth. We can write it as 100th. The 100th comes next after the 99th.

2 If you are dealing with fractions one hundredth is $\frac{1}{100}$ or 1 part of something that's been divided into 100 equal parts.

$\frac{100}{100} = 1$ whole $\frac{50}{100} = \frac{1}{2}$ $\frac{25}{100} = \frac{1}{4}$ $\frac{10}{100} = \frac{1}{10}$

hypotenuse

The hypotenuse is the longest side of a right-angled triangle. It is the side opposite the right angle.

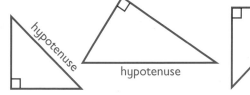

a
b
c
d
e
f
g
h
li
j
k
l
m
n
o
p
q
r
s
t
u
v
w
x
y
z

identical

Things that are identical are exactly the same as each other. The legs of a chair need to be of identical lengths – if they aren't the chair will wobble.

If two shapes are identical they are exactly the same size, shape and orientation. ('The same orientation' means that they are the same way round – they face the same way.) Identical shapes match in every way.

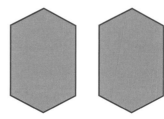

identify

If you have to identify something you pick it out and name it or explain it in some way. Here are some examples.

Identify the largest number in this list: 3 19 45 8 35. The answer is 45.

Identify this shape.

The answer is a square.

You might have to identify something like the wettest week on a weather chart, the cheapest shopping list or the shortest route from one place to another on a map.

imperial units

Imperial units used to be the standard measurements in Britain. We still use some of them. These are the ones you are most likely to meet:

Length		Capacity
12 inches (in)	= 1 foot (ft)	8 pints = 1 gallon
3 feet (ft)	= 1 yard (yd)	
1760 yards (yd)	= 1 mile	
Mass		
16 ounces (oz)	= 1 pound (lb)	
14 pounds (lb)	= 1 stone (st)	

There is some more information that might be useful to you under **capacity**, **length** and **mass**. You can find the metric measurements under **metric units**.

improbable

If something is improbable it is not likely. It's not impossible – but it's very unlikely. It is not impossible for a footballer to score ten goals in a match, for example, but it is improbable. (The opposite is probable: likely.)

The section under **probability** might interest you.

improper fractions

These are sometimes called 'top heavy fractions'. The top number of the fraction is greater than the bottom number.

$$\frac{3}{2} \quad \frac{7}{4} \quad \frac{8}{4} \quad \frac{13}{10}$$

These are all improper fractions.
They are worth more than one whole so they can also be written as mixed numbers:

$$\frac{3}{2} = 1\frac{1}{2} \qquad \frac{7}{4} = 1\frac{3}{4}$$

If you need to know more about them look up **fractions**.

inch

An inch is a measurement of length in the imperial system.

This line ——————— is one inch long.

12 inches	= 1 foot
3 feet	= 1 yard

In metric measurements: 1 inch is about 2·5cm ($2\frac{1}{2}$ cm)
                         1 foot is about 30cm.

increase

If something is increased there is more of it. If people get a pay increase they earn **more** money – something is added on to their pay. If you increase your score in a game by 10, you add 10 on to it.

We might talk about an increase in weight, increasing amounts of traffic on the roads, price increases and so on.

integer

An integer is a whole number. It can be any of the whole numbers we use for counting including 0, positive numbers and negative numbers.

interior

The interior is the inside.
The interior angles of a triangle
are the three angles inside it.
The three interior angles of a
triangle always add up to 180°.
(The opposite is **exterior**,
meaning outside.)

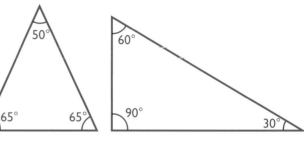

International Date Line

(Look up **Greenwich Mean Time** if you need to know about that.)
The International Date Line is drawn from the North Pole to the South
Pole, on the opposite side of the world from Greenwich in London.
If people cross the line when they are travelling towards the west, they
have to put the date forward a day. If people cross the line when they
are travelling towards the east, they have to put the date back a day.

People who travel across the International Date Line could move from
– say – Monday back to Sunday, or from Sunday to Monday depending
on the direction they were going in.

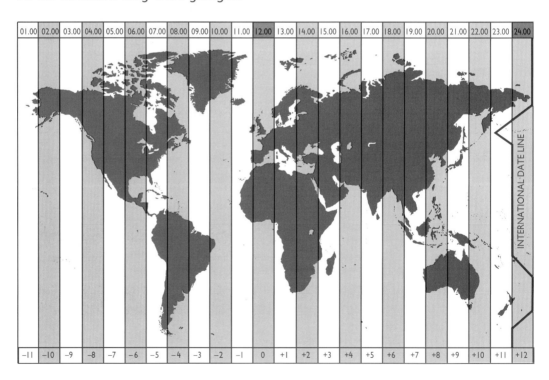

If you look on a map or a globe that has the International Date Line
marked on it you'll see that it is not a straight line, as you would
expect. That is because the line has been drawn to avoid land as far
as possible. This is easier to understand if you look at it on a globe.

intersect intersection

Intersecting lines cross each other. They intersect.

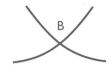

These lines intersect at A.   These arcs intersect at B.

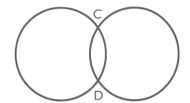

These circles intersect at C and D.

A, B, C and D show the points of intersection – the points where the lines cross each other.

Ring pictures often have intersecting rings. Look at this one.

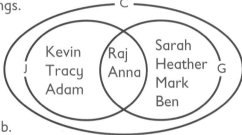

The children in ring C all live in the same road.
The children in ring J go to the judo club.
The children in ring G go to the gym club.
Raj and Anna go to both clubs. They are members of both clubs so the rings intersect.
(Ring pictures are also called **Venn Diagrams**.)

inverse

The inverse of something is the opposite.
The inverse of addition is subtraction.

4 + 8 = 12

12 − 8 = 4

The inverse of multiplication is division.

5 × 2 = 10   10 ÷ 2 = 5

The inverse of $\frac{2}{3}$ is $\frac{3}{2}$.

a
b
c
d
e
f
g
h
Ii
Jj
k
l
m
n
o
p
q
r
s
t
u
v
w
x
y
z

investigate

If you have to investigate something, you see what you can find out about it. You look into it. It's often a good idea to start jotting things down as you find them out. It helps you to remember everything.

You might have to write down the results of your investigation later, so that other people can read about it – or you might have to explain it to someone.

isosceles triangle

(Say 'I-sosser-leez'.) An isosceles triangle is a 2D shape with 3 sides.

It has 2 sides of equal length and it has 2 equal angles.

It has 1 line of symmetry.

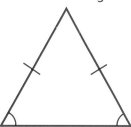  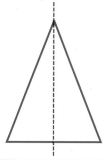

justify

If you have to justify an answer you have given, you have to explain why you think it is right.

kilo-

Kilo- comes from the Greek word for a thousand.

kilogram

A kilogram (kg) is a metric measure of mass (or weight).

1 kilogram	=	1000 grams (g)
A half-kilogram	=	500 grams
$\frac{1}{4}$ kilogram	=	250 grams

A kilogram is about 2·2 lbs (pounds) in the imperial system of measuring.

There is some more information that might be useful to you under **mass** and **weight**.

kilometre

A kilometre (km) is a metric measure of length.

1 kilometre	=	1000 metres (m)
$\frac{1}{2}$ km	=	500m
$\frac{1}{4}$ km	=	250m

A kilometre is about $\frac{5}{8}$ mile in the imperial system of measuring.

(8km is about 5 miles.)

kite

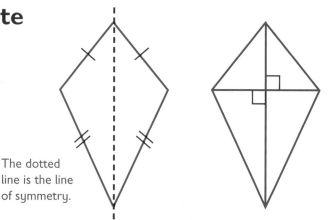

The dotted line is the line of symmetry.

In maths a kite is a quadrilateral. That means that it is a 2D shape with 4 straight sides. It has 2 equal sides next to each other and 2 longer equal sides that are also next to each other. It has one line of symmetry. The diagonals intersect at right angles.

a
b
c
d
e
f
g
h
i
j
k
Ll
m
n
o
p
q
r
s
t
u
v
w
x
y
z

leap year

Most years have 365 days but a leap year has 366. The extra day is February 29th. Normally we have a leap year every fourth year. The year 2000 was a leap year. The next leap year after that is 2004.

A year is supposed to be the length of time the earth takes to go round the sun. In the time of Julius Caesar the calendar was changed to make it more accurate (nearer to being right). The year became 365 days long – but every fourth year there was to be an extra day because it takes 365 and a bit days for the earth to go round the sun. Those years were called leap years.

That worked well for a long time. Some hundreds of years later though, the calendar had become about ten days out. They sorted out the problem and started a new calendar – which we still use. We still have the extra day every four years except for one small change.

Instead of counting **all** the years that are an exact number of hundreds as leap years, we only count them as leap years if they divide exactly by 400. (If the first two digits divide exactly by 4, the whole number will divide exactly by 400.)
2000 and 2400 count as leap years, 2100, 2200 and 2300 do not.

length

The length of something tells us how long it is. We might talk about the length of a peg or a piece of string; the length of a football pitch or the length of a corridor.

Sometimes we talk about a length of **time** – or the length of time that something takes. Look up **time** if you want to know more about that.

When you are using a ruler or a tape measure look at it carefully. Some of them have a blank piece at the end in case the corners get damaged. This bit is called the waste end. Make sure you start measuring from the beginning of the first centimetre (or inch).

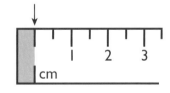

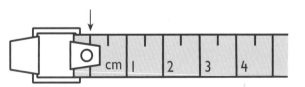

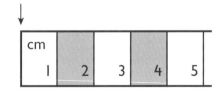

You can measure a curve with the help of a piece of string. Hold one end of the string at the beginning of the line, then curve it on top of the line a little bit at a time. Pinching both ends of the string, pull it straight and use the ruler to measure it. It won't give an exact measurement but if you are careful you shouldn't be far out.

Think whether it's sensible to measure in millimetres, centimetres or metres and what to use. Metre sticks or surveyors' long tapes can be useful for measuring the longer amounts.

The metric measures of length are:

10 millimetres (mm)	=	1 centimetre (cm)
100 centimetres (cm)	=	1 metre (m)
1000 metres (m)	=	1 kilometre (km)

The imperial measurements of length are:

12 inches (in)	=	1 foot (ft)
3 feet (ft)	=	1 yard (yd)
1760 yards	=	1 mile

(There are a few more but you are not very likely to come across them.)

Imperial and metric equivalents:
1 inch is about 2·5 centimetres.
1 foot is about 30 centimetres.
1 metre is about 39 inches (3 inches more than a yard)
1 kilometre is about $\frac{5}{8}$ mile.
(8 kilometres is about 5 miles.)

less

Less means fewer, not as many.
3 less than 5 is 2.

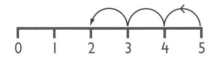 $5 - 3 = 2$

6 is one less than 7.
6 is one hundred less than 106.
£12 less £4 = £12 − £4 = £8.

< stands for **is less than**.
  3 < 5   means 3 is less than 5.
  6 < 10   means 6 is less than 10.
  ☐ < 12   means that the missing number is less than 12.

The opposite is **>** which stands for **is greater than** or **is more than**. Think of the sign as a hungry mouth. It opens towards the greater amount.
5 > 3 (5 is greater than 3)   3 < 5 (3 is less than 5)

lines

You should have a good point on your pencil whenever you draw a line because really it should have no width at all! It has only one measurement and that is its own length.

When you need to draw straight lines you usually need to use a ruler. If you have to draw a line between two points you have to draw it from one point to the other. You join them up.

There are hints about measuring straight lines and curved lines in the section on **length**.

Look up some of these words if you want to know about different kinds of lines: **diagonal**, **graphs** (for line graphs), **horizontal**, **vertical**, **parallel lines**, **perpendicular**, **symmetry** (for lines of symmetry).

likelihood

What is the likelihood of something happening? This means – how likely is it to happen? What are the chances of it happening?

Look up **probability** if you want to know more about this.

litre

We can buy litres of lemonade, litres of milk, litres of ice cream, litres of petrol and so on. We can also measure the amount that a container can **hold** in litres. This is called a measure of **capacity**.

1 litre (l)	=	1000 millilitres (ml)
A half-litre	=	500 millilitres (ml)
$\frac{1}{4}$ litre	=	250 millilitres (ml)

1 litre is about $1\frac{3}{4}$ pints (1·75 pints)

$4\frac{1}{2}$ litres (4·5 litres) are about 1 gallon (8 pints).

long division

Long division is a way of writing down a division calculation so that you can work out a bit at a time – and it's easy to see all the working out as you go along. There is more than one method of doing this. There are some examples near the end of the section on **division**.

long multiplication

We can use long multiplication when we are multiplying by numbers greater than 10. If you are not sure about multiplication with numbers less than 10 look up **multiplication** and read it carefully.

When we need to multiply by numbers that are more than 10 our tables don't go far enough and it's not always easy to manage in one line of working. If we split it up into bits we can do a bit at a time. Long multiplication is no harder than ordinary multiplication – it just takes a bit longer.

For 32 x 14 we can work out   32 x 10

and   32 x 4

and add the two results together.

You can work it out just as well this way.

$$
\begin{array}{rr}
32 & 32 \\
\times\ 10 & \times\ \ 4 \\
\hline
320 & 128
\end{array}
\qquad
\begin{array}{r}
320 \\
+\ 128 \\
\hline
448
\end{array}
$$

Long multiplication is a neat way of setting this out.

$$
\begin{array}{r}
32 \\
\times\ \ 14 \\
\hline
320 \\
128 \\
\hline
448
\end{array}
$$

   320   (This row is 32 x 10)
   128   (This row is 32 x 4)
   448   (This row is 32 x 14)

To multiply   146 by 24

we work out   146 x 20 then 146 x 4 and add the results together.

$$
\begin{array}{r}
146 \\
\times\ \ 24 \\
\hline
2920 \\
584 \\
\hline
3504
\end{array}
$$

   2920   (This row is 146 x 20)
    584   (This row is 146 x 4)
   3504   (This row is 146 x 24)

(Do remember to keep your rows and columns straight.)

Here is another way of multiplying bigger numbers:
You might like to use the grid layout which sets out the calculation in a different way. The numbers are partitioned and each part of the calculation is dealt with separately.
This is how you would set out 32 x 14 in the grid.

x	30	2		
10	300	20	=	320
4	120	8	=	128
				448

This section will not teach you how to do long multiplication but it should remind you what it is if you have forgotten.

loss

If shopkeepers buy something for 30p and sell it for 25p they have made a loss. They are worse off than when they started.
They spent 30p.
They got 25p back.
Their loss was 5p. (30p − 25p = **5p**)

a
b
c
d
e
f
g
h
i
j
k
l
Mm
n
o
p
q
r
s
t
u
v
w
x
y
z

mass

In maths we often see the word mass where we might expect the word **weight**. There is a difference between the two.

The mass of a person's body is the amount of matter in it.
The weight is a measure of the amount of pull on that body by gravity.

We talk about astronauts being 'weightless' when they have escaped from the pull of earth's gravity, but their mass hasn't changed. They are still the same people.

A lunar module has the same mass on Earth as it has on the moon. The pull of the moon's gravity is much less than the pull of earth's gravity though. It takes much less thrust to get the lunar module off the moon's surface than it does to get it off the earth's surface. It seems lighter but it has the same mass, wherever it is. This does not affect our daily lives. We weigh things for cooking, we buy our fruit and vegetables by weight and we may check our weight on the bathroom scales. To mathematicians and scientists, though, the difference between mass and weight is very important.

maximum

The maximum is the greatest possible amount; the largest possible size or quantity.
30mph is the maximum speed allowed on some roads.
A maximum thermometer shows the highest temperature that has been reached in a certain time. (The opposite is the **minimum**.)

mean

The mean is an **average** amount.
If you need to find the mean of a list of numbers:
1 Add up all the numbers in the list.
2 Divide the answer by the number of numbers in the list.

Here is an example:
Find the mean of 4 1 3 2 10.
1 Add them all up: $4 + 1 + 3 + 2 + 10 = 20$
2 There are 5 numbers in the list, so divide the answer by 5.
   $20 \div 5 = 4$

The mean is 4.

To find the mean height of a group of children you would add up the height of each child and then divide the answer by the number of children in the group.
There are two other kinds of average: the **median** and the **mode**.
Look them up if you need to be reminded about them.

measurement

Taking measurements often means measuring things – or people – to find out what size they are. We measure things when we want to know how long they are, how wide, how tall, how high and so on.
We may also measure things when we want to compare sizes.
We might use a ruler, a tape measure, a metre stick, or a trundle wheel when we are measuring length. If we want to know the weight or measure the mass of something we use scales or balances, depending on what we are weighing.

To find out how much something holds we might use a measuring jug. That is a container for the measurement of capacity. For measurements of time we use clocks or watches. For measurements of angles we use a protractor. (It is sometimes called an angle measurer.)

There is a lot of information that might interest you in this book.
Try looking up some of these: **length** (with some hints on measuring), **capacity**, **metric units**, **imperial units**, **protractor**, **time**, **mass**.

median

This word is used in two different ways. You are most likely to need this one. This median is a special sort of average.

To find the median of a list of numbers:
1 Arrange the numbers in order of size.
2 Find the **middle** one.
That is the median.
Look at these examples:

Find the median of   8   5   5   6   10
1 Arrange the numbers in order of size: 5   5   **6**   8   10
2 The middle number is **6**.
The median is 6.

Look at this list of numbers though.
Find the median of   12   5   10   3   9   1
1 Arrange the numbers in order of size: 1   3   5   9   10   12
There are **two** numbers in the middle: **5** and **9**.
2 Add the two middle numbers together and divide the answer by 2.
(That gives you a number that's half-way between them.)
    5 + 9 = 14   14 ÷ 2 = 7
The median is 7.

Now for the other kind of median:
A median is also the name for a straight line drawn from the tip of an angle of a triangle to the middle of the opposite side.

The line AB is a median

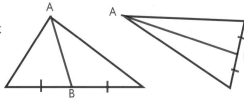

Mm

method

A method is a way of doing something. We might talk about a method of making a cake for example, or a method of working out a problem.

If you have to explain your method of doing something you have to explain how you did it – how you thought it through and how you worked it out. You explain your way of doing it.

In maths we often find different methods of getting to the right answer.

metre

A metre is the standard unit for measuring length in the metric system. The other metric measurements of length are made up from this.

See the table under **metric units** just below.
A metre is just over 39 inches in the imperial system of measuring.

metric units

The metric system is a measuring system. The metric units are based on the **metre** for measuring lengths, the **litre** for measuring capacity and the **gram** for measuring mass (or weight).

These are the most useful ones to know:

Length
10 millimetres (mm)   = 1 centimetre (cm)
100 centimetres (cm) = 1 metre (m)
1000 metres (m)   = 1 kilometre (km)

Mass
1000 milligrams (mg) = 1 gram (g)
1000 grams (g)   = 1 kilogram (kg)

Capacity
1000 millilitres (ml)   = 1 litre (l)
100 centilitres (cl)   = 1 litre

Area
100 square millimetres (mm^2)   = 1 square centimetre (cm^2)
10 000 square centimetres (cm^2) = 1 square metre (m^2)

mile

A mile is an imperial measure of distance or length.
1760 yards = 1 mile.

mph stands for miles per hour.
30 mph means a speed of 30 miles per hour.

1 kilometre (the metric measure of length or distance) is about $\frac{5}{8}$ of a mile.
(8 kilometres is about 5 miles.)

millennium

A millennium is a period of a thousand years.

milli-

Words beginning with milli- have something to do with a thousand. (It comes from mille – the Latin word for a thousand.)

1000 milligrams (mg) = 1 gram (g)

1000 millilitres (ml) = 1 litre (l)

10 millimetres = 1 centimetre (cm)
1000 millimetres (mm) = 1 metre (m)

1000 x 1000 = 1 million
10 x 10 x 10 x 10 x 10 x 10 = 1 million

milligram

A milligram is a metric measure of mass.

millilitre

A millilitre is a measure of capacity in the metric system.

millimetre

A millimetre is a measure of length in the metric system.

million

A million is a thousand thousands.
1 million is written as 1 000 000.

minimum

The minimum is the least possible, the lowest possible, the smallest possible amount.
A minimum thermometer shows the lowest temperature that has been reached in a certain time. (The opposite is the **maximum**.)

minus

The minus sign is written like this: **—** It means *less* or *take away*.

10 minus 4 means 10   4.
10 − 4 = 6

£5 minus £2 means £5 − £2.
£5 − £2 = £3

(Negative numbers have a minus sign before them, e.g. − 4   − 5 but in maths we call this 'negative 4' or 'negative 5'. We only say 'minus 4' 'minus 5' and so on when we are talking about temperatures.)
You may want to look up **subtraction** (taking away) or **negative numbers** for more information.

minute

(Say 'minit'.) A minute is a measurement of time.

> 60 seconds = 1 minute (min)
> 60 minutes = 1 hour (hr)

mirror line

Look at these shapes and the dotted lines.

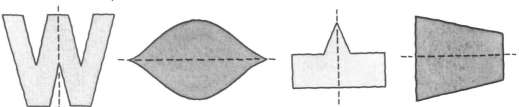

If a shape can be divided into two matching halves like this, one half 'mirrors' the other. The dividing line is called a mirror line.

If you hold a mirror so that it stands on that mirror line, it looks as if you can still see the whole shape – just as it was before. You see a reflection of half of the shape in the mirror.

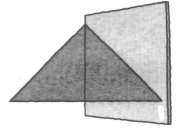

Some shapes have more than one mirror line. Look at these, the mirror lines have been marked in.

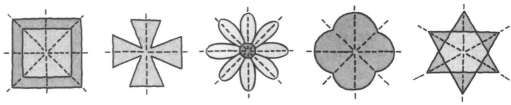

If no mirror line is marked on a shape, a mirror may help you to see if it is possible to put one (or more) in.

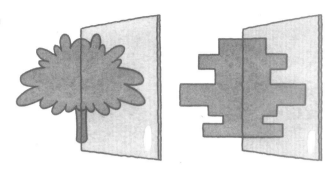

Some shapes don't have a mirror line at all. Look at these.

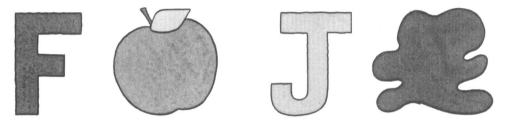

A mirror line is also called a **line of symmetry** or an **axis of symmetry**.

Sometimes you may need to draw the reflection of a shape in a mirror line. If you want a reminder about this look up **reflective symmetry**.

mixed numbers

A mixed number is a whole number with a fraction.

$3\frac{1}{2}$ $4\frac{5}{8}$ $7\frac{3}{8}$ are all mixed numbers.

Look up **fractions** if you need to know more about this.

mode

The mode is a special kind of average. To find the mode in a list of numbers look for the number – or numbers – that appear most often in the list.

Here is an example: **6 5 7 3 5 4 5 8**
5 appears three times in the list. The other numbers only appear once.
The mode is 5.

Now look at this example: **9 2 4 5 2 3 9 1 6**
9 appears twice, 2 appears twice, the other numbers only appear once.
The modes are 2 and 9.

There are two other kinds of average, **median** and **mean**. Look them up if you need to know about them.

a
b
c
d
e
f
g
h
i
j
k
l
Mm
n
o
p
q
r
s
t
u
v
w
x
y
z

a
b
c
d
e
f
g
h
i
j
k
l
Mm
n
o
p
q
r
s
t
u
v
w
x
y
z

money

(Say 'munny'.) Bank notes and coins are called money.
The notes that are used most often are the £5 note, the £10 note and the £20 note.
These are the coins that we use:

1p   5p   20p   £1

2p   10p   50p   £2

£ is the pound sign and p stands for penny or pence.

Coin	
1p	100 × 1p = £1
2p	50 × 2p = £1
5p	20 × 5p = £1
10p	10 × 10p = £1
20p	5 × 20p = £1
50p	2 × 50p = £1

We can write one penny as   1p or £0.01.
We can write five pence as   5p or £0.05.
We can write ten pence as 10p or £0.10.
We can write fifty pence as 50p or £0.50.

Remember: 100 pence (p) = £1
We can write 105p as £1.05
110p as £1.10
125p as £1.25
150p as £1.50 and so on.

When we write down money like this, the decimal point separates the pounds from the pence. There are always two digits after the point.

Buying and selling
A trader **sells** T-shirts. If someone buys one the trader has **sold** it.
When you **buy** something you **spend** some money.
When you have **bought** something you have **spent** some money.
If you don't have exactly the right money to pay for what you want you have to give a bit too much and get some **change**.
It might be useful for you to look up **amount**, **cost**, **change**, or **bills**.

Here are some words for comparing prices.

£3 each

£6 each

£12 each

This costs less than the others.

This costs more.

This costs the most.

This is the least expensive.

This is more expensive.

This is the most expensive.

This is the lowest price.

This is a higher price.

This the highest price.

This is the cheapest.

This is cheaper than the £12 ones.

This is dear.

The £6 T-shirts were more expensive than the £3 ones but they were less expensive than the £12 ones.
You may find it useful to look up some of these words:
profit, **loss**, **discount**, **currency**.

month

There are 12 months in a year:
January, February, March, April, May, June, July, August, September, October, November, December.
This rhyme helps us to remember how many days there are in each month:

Thirty days hath September,
April, June and November.
All the rest have 31,
Except February alone,
And this has 28 days clear,
But 29 in each leap year.

You might want to look up **calendar** or **leap year**.

mph

This stands for miles per hour.
30mph means a speed of 30 miles per hour.
If you travelled at 30mph for two hours you would have gone 60 miles.
(30 miles in each hour.)
Look up **distance** and **speed** if you want to know more about this.

a b c d e f g h i j k l **Mm** n o p q r s t u v w x y z

a
b
c
d
e
f
g
h
i
j
k
l
Mm
n
o
p
q
r
s
t
u
v
w
x
y
z

multiples

| 2 x 3 = 6 | 2 x 4 = 8 | 2 x 5 = 10 | 2 x 6 = 12 |

6 is a multiple of 2.
8 10 and 12 are all multiples of 2.
2 will divide exactly into any of them.

12 16 20 24 40 are all multiples of 4.
4 will divide exactly into any of them.

25 30 35 55 100 are all multiples of 5.
5 will divide exactly into any of them.

Multiples of any number can be divided exactly by that number.
6, 12 and 18 are all **common** multiples of 2 and 3.
2 and 3 are common factors of 6, 12 and 18.
2 and 3 will both divide exactly into any of them.
The lowest (least) common multiple of 2 and 3 is 6.
6 is the lowest common multiple of 2 and 3 because it is the smallest number that they will both divide into exactly.

---

multiplication

The sign for multiplication is **x**.
2 x 3 means 2 *multiplied by* 3. We can also say 2 *times* 3.
Multiplication is a quick way of adding up equal groups of things.
Look at these examples:

 3 lots of 3 = 3 x 3   3 x 3 = 9

 4 lots of 2 = 4 x 2   4 x 2 = 8

Look at these rows and columns.

Two rows of 4 come to the same as four columns of 2.

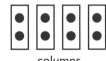

rows   columns

Here are 5 packets of buns with 4 in each packet. How many buns are there altogether?

You could add 4 + 4 + 4 + 4 + 4 together like this:
    4 + 4 = 8   (That's 2 fours)
and 4 more = 12   (That's 3 fours)

and 4 more = 16   (That's 4 fours)
and 4 more = **20**   (That's 5 fours.)
There are 20 buns altogether.
(That is sometimes called repeated addition.)
You could multiply: 5 x 4 = 20.
If you know the multiplication tables this way is much quicker.

A **multiplication table** is a list of equal groups already
counted up. They usually go up to 10 x the number.

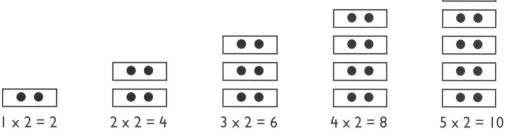

| 1 x 2 = 2 | 2 x 2 = 4 | 3 x 2 = 6 | 4 x 2 = 8 | 5 x 2 = 10 |

That is how the 2 x table is built up.

The 3 x table counts up groups
of three.

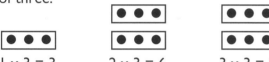

| 1 x 3 = 3 | 2 x 3 = 6 | 3 x 3 = 9 | and so on. |

This is a multiplication square. It shows
lists of tables already worked out.
(Look up page 190 for more about
these.)

It really is worth learning the
multiplication tables. Once you know
them you can save yourself such a lot
of time. When you really know them
well your brain can punch out the
answers faster than your fingers can
use a calculator!

1	2	3	4	5	6	7	8	9	10
2	4	6	8	10	12	14	16	18	20
3	6	9	12	15	18	21	24	27	30
4	8	12	16	20	24	28	32	36	40
5	10	15	20	25	30	35	40	45	50
6	12	18	24	30	36	42	48	54	60
7	14	21	28	35	42	49	56	63	70
8	16	24	32	40	48	56	64	72	80
9	18	27	36	45	54	63	72	81	90
10	20	30	40	50	60	70	80	90	100

multiply

To multiply is to increase something a number of times.
Multiplying is multiplication. The sign we use is **X**.

To multiply 4 by 2 you work out 4 x 2   **4 x 2 = 8**   (It is 4 two times.)

We could also say multiply 4 by 2 as 4 times 2 or the product of 4 and
2 or two lots of 4. They would all have the same answer.
If you want to know more about this read **multiplication**.

a
b
c
d
e
f
g
h
i
j
k
l
m

o
p
q
r
s
t
u
v
w
x
y
z

necessary

If something is necessary it is needed – or it needs to be done. If you want to draw a straight line, a pencil and ruler may be necessary. It may be necessary to count up your money before you go out to buy something.

If you want to write 'necessary', it is necessary to be able to spell it! In this word the **c** and the **ss** sound the same and a lot of people forget which comes first and how many there are of each letter. Think of the alphabet: c comes before s. Think of counting: 1 comes before 2. The word is **ne_c_e_ss_ary**. (Say 'ne-ce-ssary'.)

negative numbers

Numbers that are less than zero are called negative numbers. Negative numbers have a minus sign in front of them. −1 is a negative number. It is one less than zero. −2 is two less than zero.

Look along the number line. We count the negative numbers back from zero like this: negative 1, negative 2, negative 3, negative 4 and so on.

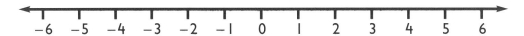

(A number with a plus sign before it is called a positive number. It is above zero. If there is no sign before a number it is always counted as positive.)

net

This word has two meanings that you might come across in maths. They are quite different.

1 One meaning of the word net is a flat shape which can be cut out and folded up to make a 3D shape.

This shape is a net for making an open cube. You can see which part will be the base and which parts will make the sides when they are folded up.

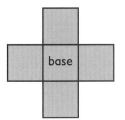

This net would make an open cube too.

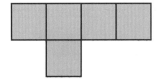

This net would make a closed cube. You can see that it will have a base, 4 sides and a top.

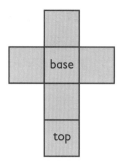

These nets would make closed cubes too. (You may be able to draw some more.)

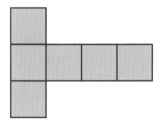 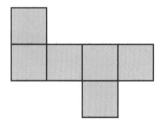 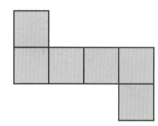

This net would make a cuboid.

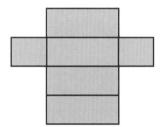 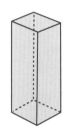

This net would make a regular tetrahedron.

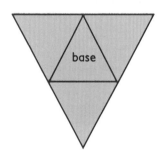 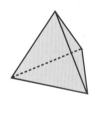

2 Another meaning of the word net is to do with amounts of things. After a school fete someone might say, 'The net profit is £150.' The **net profit** is the amount of money left after they have paid all the expenses of running the fete.

The **net weight** of something is the amount it weighs, not counting the weight of any wrappings or packaging.

nonagon

A nonagon is a 2D shape with 9 sides and 9 angles.
If all of the sides and all of the angles are equal it is a regular nonagon.

noon

Noon is 12 o'clock in the daytime (12:00). It is midday.

nought

A nought is written as 0. It means none – not any. In maths we usually call it zero. 0 can be a starting point for measuring or on a number line.

If you want to know more about this look up **zero**. The sections on **place value** or **decimals** might be useful to you as well.

number bonds

Number bonds are the pairs of whole numbers that will make up another number.
These are the number bonds that make up 10:

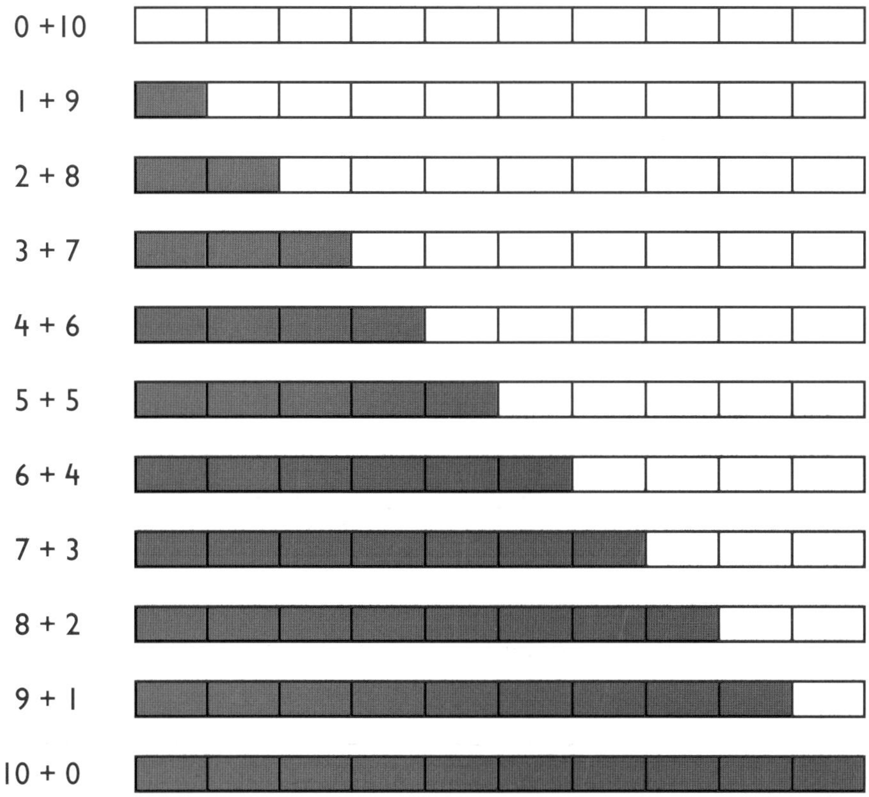

0 + 10
1 + 9
2 + 8
3 + 7
4 + 6
5 + 5
6 + 4
7 + 3
8 + 2
9 + 1
10 + 0

number sentence

This is a number sentence:

4 + 8 = 12

A number sentence uses numbers and signs.
We could write that sentence in words. We could write:

four add eight equals twelve or **four and eight make twelve**.

A number sentence is much quicker to write and it's easier to work with in maths. These are all number sentences:

$3 - 3 = 0$ $10 \times 10 = 100$ $6 \times 1 = 3 \times 2$

$14 \div 2 = 7$ $7 - 3 = 8 - 4$ $\frac{1}{2} + \frac{1}{2} + \frac{1}{2} = 1\frac{1}{2}$

$12 = 7 + 5$ $27 = 3 \times 9$

Sometimes one of the numbers in a number sentence is missing. There may be an empty box in the place where it should be. You may have to find the missing number. Look at these examples:

$19 - \square = 17$ $\square \times 5 = 20$
$19 - 2 = 17$ $4 \times 5 = 20$
The missing number is 2.   The missing number is 4.

You may have to find a missing sign.
The missing sign might be $+$ or $-$ or $\times$ or $\div$.

$18 \square 2 = 9$
$18 \div 2 = 9$
The missing sign is $\div$.

Sometimes there is a letter in the place where the missing number should be. Look at this example:

$x + 6 = 8$
$2 + 6 = 8$
$x = 2$

Sometimes more than one number is missing. Look at this example:

$\triangle + \square = 12$

There are lots of possible answers for this. You could use any two numbers that make up 12.

Look up **signs** and **symbols** if you want to know more about them.

---

numeral

A numeral is a number written in figures.

---

numerator

The numerator is the top number of a fraction.

$\frac{3}{5}$ In this fraction the numerator is 3.

(The bottom number of a fraction is called the denominator.)
Look up **fractions** if you want to know more about this.

a
b
c
d
e
f
g
h
i
j
k
l
m
n
Oo
p
q
r
s
t
u
v
w
x
y
z

oblong

An oblong is a 2D shape which has 4 straight sides. Its angles are all right angles, it has two pairs of parallel sides and its opposite sides are equal to each other in length. The sides which are next to each other are **not** equal though. An oblong is a rectangle but it is never a square.

An oblong has 2 lines of symmetry.

Look up **rectangle** if you want a reminder about that.

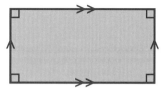
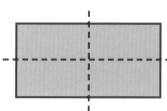

obtuse angle

Obtuse angles are more than 90° but less than 180°.

Look up **angles** If you want to know more about them.

octagon

An octagon is a 2D shape with 8 sides and 8 angles. If the sides and angles are all equal it is a called a regular octagon.

regular octagon   irregular octagon

octagonal

Something which is octagonal has 8 sides. It is shaped like an octagon.

octahedron   (The plural is octahedra.)

An octahedron is a 3D shape with 8 faces. This diagram shows a regular octahedron: each face is an equilateral triangle.

You may be interested to look up **polyhedron**.

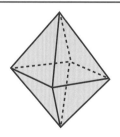

odd numbers

Odd numbers are whole numbers that can't be divided exactly by 2. If you divide an odd number by 2 there is always 1 left over.

 1 is an odd number

 2 is an even number

$3 \div 2 = 1$ and 1 is left over.   3 is an odd number.

$4 \div 2 = 2$ exactly.   4 is an even number.

$5 \div 2 = 2$ and 1 is left over.   5 is an odd number.

Odd numbers always end in   1, 3, 5, 7 or 9.

These are all odd numbers: **9   21   305   4169**

If you add 2 odd
numbers together
they always make
an even number.

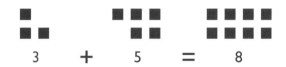

3   **+**   5   **=**   8

---

once

(Say 'wunce'.) If you do something once you do it just one
time. If you do it **once more** after that, you have done it
one more time – you have done it **twice**.

---

order   ordering

If you have to order a list of numbers, you have to put them
in order. Unless you are told something different you start
with the lowest and finish with the highest.
Look at these numbers:

316   27   1000   120   6

To order them, write down the lowest number in the list first. It is 6.

Then look at the rest of the numbers. 27 comes next.

Look at the rest of the numbers to find which one comes after 27 and
write that down.
Keep doing this until you have written down the last number. (That will
be the highest one in the list.)

The ordered list will look like this:

6   27   120   316   1000

It goes from the lowest to highest.

More ...

a
b
c
d
e
f
g
h
i
j
k
l
m
n
Oo
p
q
r
s
t
u
v
w
x
y
z

a
b
c
d
e
f
g
h
i
j
k
l
m
n
Oo
p
q
r
s
t
u
v
w
x
y
z

Sometimes it may not be easy to see which number comes next. Try jotting them down underneath each other. Make sure you put the units under the units, the tens under the tens, the hundreds under the hundreds and so on. (Put them under the headings if it helps you.) Then you may find it easier to pick them out in the right order.

Sometimes you have to order a list of things starting with the **largest**. Look at the list and write down the largest one first. Then look at the rest to see which comes next. (It will be the next largest.) Keep doing that and writing them down until you have put the whole list in order.

Here is an example.

101   4   78   1250   621

If we order these numbers *starting with the largest* they would look like this:

1250   621   101   78   4

You may have to order negative numbers. Look at these:

−12   −4   −20   −18

Starting with the lowest number the order would be:

−20   −18   −12   −4

You might have to arrange them along a number line.

Ascending order or descending order
You may have to arrange things in ascending order or descending order. Ascending means going up, so you put them in order with the lowest amount first, then the next and so on until you get to the highest. That is the last in the list.

Descending means going down, so you put them in order starting with the highest amount and ending with the lowest amount.

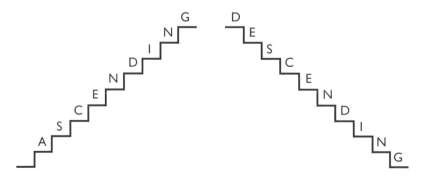

Remember: ascending is going up and descending is going down.

> **Useful words to remember:**
>
> | going down | descending | getting smaller | decreasing |
> | lowest | least | smallest | |
> | | | | |
> | going up | ascending | getting bigger | increasing |
> | highest | largest | biggest | greatest |

If you have to **rearrange** things you have to change them around – you have to put them in a different order.

Ordering different kinds of things

It may not always be numbers that you have to put in order: you use the same ways of working to order other kinds of things such as measurements or amounts of money.

Put these amounts of money in order, greatest first:
£5.35   £2.75   £2.50   £3.05

The order would be:
£5.35   £3.05   £2.75   £2.50

Order these amounts of money, smallest first:
£4.00   35p   £3.50   500p   £2

The order would be:
35p   £2   £3.50   £4.00   500p

(Don't forget that 500p = £5.00)

Arrange these in ascending order:
$3\frac{1}{4}$ $\frac{3}{4}$ $\frac{1}{2}$ $2\frac{1}{2}$ $\frac{1}{4}$

The order would be:
$\frac{1}{4}$ $\frac{1}{2}$ $\frac{3}{4}$ $2\frac{1}{2}$ $3\frac{1}{4}$

(To put different kinds of fractions in order you may need to change them to the same kind. Then it is easier to compare sizes. Look up **fractions** if you don't remember how to do it.)

Order these decimals, starting with the lowest:
3·05   4·31   3·15   4·02

The order would be:
3·05   3·15   4·02   4·31

(Sometimes it may not be easy to see which decimal comes next. Try jotting them down underneath each other – but remember to keep the decimal points under each other. That will keep all the digits in the right places. Then you may find it easier to see how to sort them out.)

More ...

Order these percentages, starting with the highest:
25%   20%   100%   10%   1%

The order would be:
100%   25%   20%   10%   1%

Now rearrange them to start with the lowest:
The new order would be:
1%   10%   20%   25%   100%

---

ounce

Ounces are part of the imperial system of weights.

16 ounces (oz) = 1 pound (lb)

(These pounds have nothing to do with money.)

> 16 oz = 1 lb
>
> 12 oz = $\frac{3}{4}$ lb
>
> 8 oz = $\frac{1}{2}$ lb
>
> 4 oz = $\frac{1}{4}$ lb

One ounce weighs about 30 grams in the metric system.
(28 grams is a bit nearer if you need to be more accurate.)

---

outcome

The outcome of something is the result. It might be the result of
something that has happened or something that has been tried out.
The outcome is something that has 'come out of it'.
If you have been trying something out in maths you might tell people
what you have found out. That would be the outcome of your work.

---

oval

Ovals are curved 2D shapes but they are not
round like circles. They look like circles that have
been stretched. An oval is also called an ellipse.

p.m. (pm)

This stands for post meridiem – Latin words meaning after midday, afternoon. 5pm means 5 o'clock in the afternoon.

On the 24 hour clock 5pm is shown as 17:00
(5**am** (ante meridiem) means 5 o'clock in the morning.)
If you want to know more about this, look up **time** or the
twenty-four hour clock.

parallel lines

Parallel lines are the same distance apart from each other all the way along their length. Even if you make them longer they will never meet.

On diagrams parallel lines are often shown with little arrow heads marked on them, like this:

parallelogram

A parallelogram is a four-sided 2D shape with its opposite sides parallel to each other. (The opposite sides are also equal to each other in length.)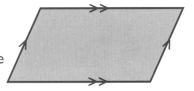

partition

A partition might be pulled across a hall to divide it into two smaller rooms. It would separate one part from the other.

Partitioning in maths works in much the same way.
You could partition 10 into 5 + 5 or 6 + 4 and so on.

Partition 58 means separate the parts – split it up.
58 is 5 tens and 8 units. If you partition 58 into tens and units, you get 50 + 8.

If you partition 436 into hundreds, tens, and units you get 400 + 30 + 6.

Partitioning can sometimes give you a quick way of working things out. Look at these examples:

For 52 + 57 you could work out: $(50 + 50) + (2 + 7) = 100 + 9 = 109$

For 26 x 3 you could work out: $(20 \times 3) + (6 \times 3) = 60 + 18 = 78$

You can partition numbers in all sorts of ways. For example 47 can be partitioned into 40 + 7 or 30 + 17 or 42 + 5 and so on.

a
b
c
d
e
f
g
h
i
j
k
l
m
n
o
Pp
q
r
s
t
u
v
w
x
y
z

pattern

In maths we often find patterns of numbers and patterns of shapes.
Sometimes the same pattern is repeated over and over again.

A pattern can be made with, for example,
tiles, circles or coloured pegs.

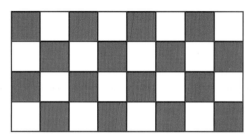

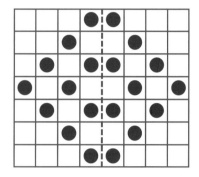

You can make lots of different counting patterns on grids.
This one was made by counting up in threes.

1	2	3	4	5	6	7	8	9	10
11	12	13	14	15	16	17	18	19	20
21	22	23	24	25	26	27	28	29	30
31	32	33	34	35	36	37	38	39	40
41	42	43	44	45	46	47	48	49	50
51	52	53	54	55	56	57	58	59	60
61	62	63	64	65	66	67	68	69	70
71	72	73	74	75	76	77	78	79	80
81	82	83	84	85	86	87	88	89	90
91	92	93	94	95	96	97	98	99	100

Sometimes you may have to find some missing numbers in a sequence.

Something like: **7   11   15   19**   ☐   ☐

If you find the pattern in the sequence you can carry on with the same
pattern to fill in the missing numbers.
Look to see how you can get from each number to the next one.

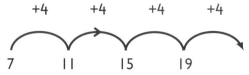

To carry on with this pattern you find 19 + 4 to get the next number: 23.
Then 23 + 4 to find the next one: 27.
The missing numbers in this sequence are 23 and 27.

Quite often it takes a bit longer before you can see the pattern in the numbers. Look up **sequence** if you want to see some more examples. You might be interested to look up the patterns in **square numbers** and **triangular numbers** as well.

People sometimes talk about a pattern of work. It means work that has been planned out so that it can be done in the same way over and over again.

You might be interested to look up **formula**. A formula gives us a pattern for working something out.

pentagon

A pentagon is a 2D shape which has 5 sides and 5 angles. If all of the sides and angles are equal it is called a regular pentagon.

regular pentagon   irregular pentagon

pentagonal

If something is pentagonal it is shaped like a pentagon.

percentages

Per cent means **for every hundred** or **out of a hundred**. The sign for per cent is **%**.

Here are 100 squares.

3 squares out of the hundred are shaded.

$\frac{3}{100}$ are shaded.

$\frac{3}{100}$ can be called 3 per cent. We write it as 3%.

3% of the squares are shaded.

97 of the squares are not shaded.

$\frac{97}{100}$ are not shaded.

$\frac{97}{100}$ can be called 97 per cent. We write it as 97%.

3% of the squares are shaded.
97% of the squares are unshaded.

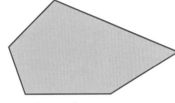

$\frac{1}{100} = 1\%$ $\frac{2}{100} = 2\%$ $\frac{3}{100} = 3\%$ $\frac{24}{100} = 24\%$ $\frac{36}{100} = 36\%$ $\frac{74}{100} = 74\%$

More ...

a b c d e f g h i j k l m n o **Pp** q r s t u v w x y z

percentages

A boy had 56% for a Maths test. This means that he had 56 marks out of 100. $56\% = \frac{56}{100}$

If someone had 100% it would mean that they had $\frac{100}{100}$ They had no mistakes at all.

$100\% = \frac{100}{100}$ 100% is the whole lot.

$50\% = \frac{50}{100} = \frac{1}{2}$ $25\% = \frac{25}{100} = \frac{1}{4}$ $75\% = \frac{75}{100} = \frac{3}{4}$

It is easy to write percentages as fractions.

$10\% = \frac{10}{100} = \frac{\cancel{10}^{1}}{\cancel{100}_{10}} = \frac{1}{10}$

$20\% = \frac{20}{100} = \frac{\cancel{20}^{1}}{\cancel{100}_{5}} = \frac{1}{5}$

It is useful to learn these as we often need them:

$75\% = \frac{3}{4}$ $33\frac{1}{3}\% = \frac{1}{3}$ $20\% = \frac{1}{5}$

$50\% = \frac{1}{2}$ $66\frac{2}{3}\% = \frac{2}{3}$ $10\% = \frac{1}{10}$

$25\% = \frac{1}{4}$ $5\% = \frac{1}{20}$

12·5% or $12\frac{1}{2}\% = \frac{1}{8}$ $1\% = \frac{1}{100}$

It is also useful to learn these decimals as percentages:

0·75 = 75%   0·25 = 25%   0·1 = 10%
0·5 = 50%   0·125 = 12·5%   0·01 = 1%

Here are some examples of using percentages:

1 *What is 10% of £20?*

$10\% = \frac{10}{100} = \frac{1}{10}$

$\frac{1}{10}$ of £20 = £2 (£20 ÷ 10)

10% of £20 = £2

2 *Find 20% of 30 people.*

$20\% = \frac{\cancel{20}^{1}}{\cancel{100}_{5}} = \frac{1}{5}$

$\frac{1}{5}$ of 30 people = 6 people. (30 ÷ 5)

This way of doing it will always work, but do look out for quicker ways when you have easy numbers.

If you remember that $10\% = \frac{1}{10}$ you could say:

10% of 30 people = 3 people
20% is double 10% so 20% of 30 people = 6 people.

3 *In a sale 5% is taken off the usual price of everything in a window.*

If the usual price of something is £40,
5% of £40 is taken off the price.
Remember, 5% is half of 10% so the
quick way is to say:
10% of £40 = £4 so 5% of £40 = £2.
£2 is taken off the usual price.
The sale price is £38 (£40 − £2).

4 *Some people are to have a 4% pay rise. How much extra will people earning £12 000 a year get?*

A 4% rise means that for every £100 they earn
they will get an extra £4.

On £100   they would get £4
On £1000   they would get (10 × £4) £40
On £12 000 they will get (£12 × 40) £480
On £12 000 they will get £480 extra a year.

5 *Members of a club are offered 10% discount.*

This means that 10% is taken off their bills. (Remember 10% = $\frac{1}{10}$)
If a bill comes to £100, £10 is taken off. They pay £90.
If a bill comes to £50, £5 is taken off. They pay £45.

6 *A girl had $\frac{16}{20}$ for Maths, $\frac{15}{25}$ for English and $\frac{6}{10}$ for History.*

If you change all her marks to percentages it is easier to compare them.
To write a fraction as a percentage, change the fraction to one with a
denominator of a hundred.

    Maths $\frac{16 \,(\times 5)}{20 \,(\times 5)} = \frac{80}{100} = 80\%$

    English $\frac{15 \,(\times 4)}{25 \,(\times 4)} = \frac{60}{100} = 60\%$

    History $\frac{6 \,(\times 10)}{10 \,(\times 10)} = \frac{60}{100} = 60\%$

perimeter

The perimeter is the distance all the way round
the edge of something: the boundary.

A is a rectangular field.
Its perimeter   = (100 + 150 + 100 + 150) metres.
The perimeter = 500 metres.

B is a garden.
Its perimeter   = (8 + 12 + 15 + 8) metres.
The perimeter = 43 metres.

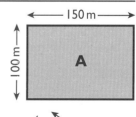

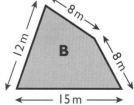

perpendicular

A line which is perpendicular to another one meets it at **right angles**.
Angle ABC is a right angle.
Angle ABD is a right angle.
The line AB is perpendicular to CD.

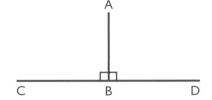

pictogram

A pictogram (or pictograph) is a kind of graph which uses little pictures or symbols to show its information.
This pictogram shows the numbers of rounders scored when children were at a camp.

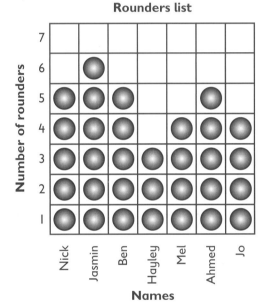

represents (stands for) 1 rounder

If you'd like to see more examples of pictograms, or some hints on drawing them, look up the section on **graphs**.
The part you need is near the beginning.

pie chart

A pie chart looks like a pie marked off into slices. This is a way of showing information. Pie charts make it easy to compare different amounts.

People travelling on a coach outing
In this chart we can see very quickly that half of the people on the outing were women and that there were not nearly as many men.

About $\frac{1}{8}$ of the people were men.

About $\frac{3}{8}$ of them were children.

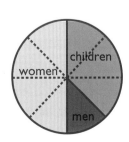

How Mark spent his pocket money

Here the pie chart is divided into 16 equal slices so one slice is $\frac{1}{16}$ of the whole lot.

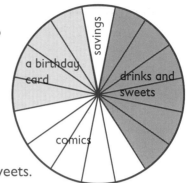

It shows that Mark saved $\frac{1}{16}$ of his money.

$\frac{6}{16}$ (or $\frac{3}{8}$) of his money was spent on drinks and sweets.

$\frac{5}{16}$ of his money was spent on comics.

$\frac{4}{16}$ (or $\frac{2}{8}$ or $\frac{1}{4}$) of his money was spent on a birthday card.

You can compare the amounts he spent on different things just by looking at the chart. If you knew how much pocket money Mark had you could work out how much he spent on each sort of thing and how much he saved.

If you are drawing a chart of your own you need to decide how big to make the slices. The whole pie stands for the whole amount you are dealing with.

Don't forget to give it a title and label it so that people understand what it's all about.

pint

Pints are a measure of capacity in the imperial system.

8 pints = 1 gallon

1 litre is about $1\frac{3}{4}$ pints

(1 pint is a bit more than $\frac{1}{2}$ litre.)

place value

The value of something is what it is worth.

	Th	H	T	U
3 is worth 3 units				3
30 is worth 3 tens			3	0
300 is worth 3 hundreds		3	0	0
3000 is worth 3 thousands	3	0	0	0

We can tell what the 3 is worth by its place in the number. Zeros keep it in the right place when there aren't any other digits to do it. Really a zero in a column just means 'we haven't got any of those'.

More ...

a b c d e f g h i j k l m n o **Pp** q r s t u v w x y z

a
b
c
d
e
f
g
h
i
j
k
l
m
n
o

Pp

q
r
s
t
u
v
w
x
y
z

301 means 3 hundreds, no tens and 1 unit.
We say: 3 hundred and one.

310 means 3 hundreds, 1 ten and no units.
We say: 3 hundred and ten.

Remember:
Th H T U
   1 0 1   101 is 1 hundred and one.
1 0 0 1   1001 is 1 thousand and one.

If you are not sure what a number is worth put the headings above the digits.

Th H T U
1 0 4 2   is 1 thousand and forty-two:
             The 1 is worth 1 thousand
             The 0 shows that there are no hundreds
             The 4 is worth 4 tens (forty).
             The 2 is worth 2 units.

1 1 4 2   is one hundred more than 1042
2 0 4 2   is one thousand more than 1042

If you are dealing with larger numbers, remember:

1	is 1 unit	
10	is 1 ten	(1 x 10)
100	is 1 hundred	(10 x 10)
1000	is 1 thousand	(100 x 10)
10 000	is 10 thousand	(1000 x 10)
100 000	is 1 hundred thousand	(10 000 x 10)
1 000 000	is 1 million	(100 000 x 10)

If you want to know about place value when you have a decimal point to deal with, look up **decimals**.

plan

If you make a plan you decide how to do something. You might plan a holiday, for example.

The word plan is also used for a special kind of drawing.
This kind of plan is often drawn as though you are directly above something, looking down. (It is sometimes called a bird's eye view.)

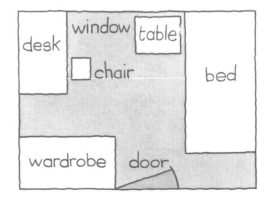

Key

P	Parking
(picnic)	Picnic area
S	Swimming
(park)	Park
(tennis)	Tennis courts
T	Toilets
H	Hospital

Often it's not possible to label everything on the plan. Numbers or symbols are used and a key shows what they stand for.

Usually a plan can't be drawn life-size. It has to fit onto a piece of paper. Everything has to be smaller than it is in real life.

If a plan is drawn to **scale** it means that everything on it has been carefully measured and made smaller in the same way. If something which is 1 metre long is drawn as 1 centimetre long we say 1 cm represents 1 m.

On that scale something which measures 2 metres in real life would be drawn 2 centimetres long. Something measuring half a metre in real life would measure half a centimetre on the plan.

Plans give an idea of the shapes and sizes of things and their positions. They can help us to find our way, to design a garden, to arrange the furniture in a room or to give directions. They can show us how the rooms of a house are arranged. They have very many uses.

When we compare different plans, though, we always have to look at the scale so that we can work out what the real life sizes or distances are. The plan for a dolls' house could be drawn the same size as a plan for a real house!

plane

A plane is a flat (2D) surface. It can be vertical, horizontal or sloping.

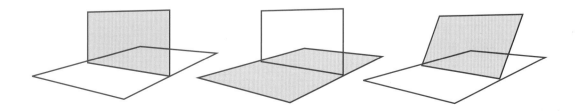

a
b
c
d
e
f
g
h
i
j
k
l
m
n
o
Pp
q
r
s
t
u
v
w
x
y
z

plot plotting

In maths plotting means marking points on a chart or a graph. If you are plotting your results you are marking them in on a chart or a graph instead of leaving them in a list. A navigator may plot a course or a route.

plus

Plus means add. We use the **+** sign.

7 plus 4 means 7 + 4.

(The plus sign by itself before a number means that it is a positive number. Look up **positive numbers** if you need to know more about this.)

polygon

(The word polygon comes from Greek. **Poly** means many and **-gon** means angle.)

A polygon is a 2D shape with a number of angles, and straight sides. If all the sides and angles are equal it is called a regular polygon.

A three-sided polygon is called a triangle. There are different kinds of triangle so look up **triangle** if you want to know more about them.

A four-sided polygon is called a quadrilateral. There are different kinds of quadrilateral, so look up **quadrilateral** if you want more details about these.

Mostly when we talk about polygons we are talking about shapes with more than four sides. Here are some special names which you might meet:

Pentagon   a 5-sided polygon.
Hexagon   a 6-sided polygon.
Heptagon   a 7-sided polygon.
Octagon   an 8-sided polygon.
Nonagon   a 9-sided polygon.
Decagon   a 10-sided polygon.
Dodecagon a 12-sided polygon.

There is a diagram of most of these shapes under their own separate headings.
(You aren't likely to need it, but just in case you wondered, an 11 sided polygon can be called an undecagon or a hendecagon. Both words mean eleven angles!)

polyhedron *(The plural is polyhedra.)*

(Say 'polly-heedron'.) A polyhedron is a 3D shape with 'many faces'.

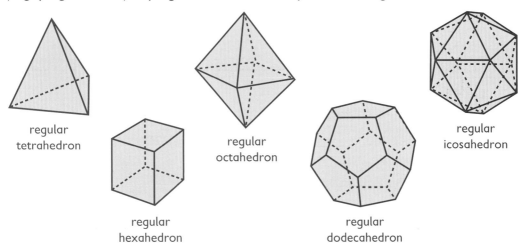

regular
tetrahedron

regular
hexahedron

regular
octahedron

regular
dodecahedron

regular
icosahedron

A corner point where faces meet is called a **vertex**.
(The plural is vertices.)

If each face is exactly the same size and shape the
polyhedron is called a regular polyhedron. There are only
five kinds of regular polyhedra:

the regular tetrahedron   which has 4 faces.
                            (Each face is an equilateral triangle.)

the regular hexahedron   which has 6 faces – we usually call this a cube.
                            (Each face is a square.)

the regular octahedron   which has 8 faces.
                            (Each face is an equilateral triangle.)

the regular dodecahedron which has 12 faces.
                            (Each face is a regular pentagon.)

the regular icosahedron   which has 20 faces.
                            (Each face is an equilateral triangle.)

(Deltahedra are polyhedra with equilateral triangles as their
faces. There are three in the list above.)

population

The people who live in a country are the population of
that country. The population of a village are the people
who live there.

The total population of a place is the number of people
living in it – all of the people counted up. The population
figures show the number of people who live there.

a
b
c
d
e
f
g
h
i
j
k
l
m
n
o
Pp
q
r
s
t
u
v
w
x
y
z

a
b
c
d
e
f
g
h
i
j
k
l
m
n
o
Pp
q
r
s
t
u
v
w
x
y
z

position

Is everyone in position? Are they ready for the game to start? Are they all in the right places?

Can you find the position of the football ground on a map?

Where did you come in the race?
What position did you come in?
Who was placed second?

If you want to know the position of something, you want to know where it is: where it has been placed, or where it has been put.

The person who wins a race comes in **first**. The next person to finish comes in **second** place, the next is in **third** place and so on. Those are their positions at the end of the race.

Here are some everyday words about the positions of things:

The biscuits are **on** the **top** shelf. You have to reach up **high** to get them. They are **above** the middle shelf. The mugs are on the **middle** shelf. The box is on the **bottom** shelf. You have to reach down **low** to get it. The box is **below** the middle shelf. The hamster is hiding **underneath** the bottom shelf.

There are lots of words about the positions of things and people:

Two girls are **outside**. They are sitting **opposite** each other. The sunshade is **over** the table. The cat is asleep **under** the table. Her dish is **beside** her. A bird is perched on the **edge** of it. The dog is **inside** the kennel, **close to** his bone!

In maths we often talk about the positions of numbers or the positions of angles.
Maps and co-ordinates can be very useful if you want to find the position of a place or if you want to tell someone else where to find it.

Changing position
If you change the position of something you move it from one place to another.

You change the positions of numbers if you put them into a special order.

The hands of a clock change position as they move round to show us the time.

The sails of a windmill change position as they rotate.

If you are thinking about positions of things there are a lot of sections in this book that could be useful to you.

There is a list of **ordinal numbers** (first, second, third, and so on) on p.188 at the back of the book.

You might also look up some of these:
order (put in order), **compass**, **co-ordinates**, **direction**, **place value**, **plan**, **rotate**, **translation**.

positive numbers

Numbers with a plus sign before them are called positive numbers.
Numbers with no sign in front of them are always counted as positive.

(Numbers which are less than zero are called negative numbers and they are written with a minus sign in front of them −1, −2, −3 and so on.)

possibility

A possibility is something which is possible, but not certain.
It **could** happen – or we **might** do it.

If there are black clouds in the sky, for example, there's a possibility that it will rain. People might have to decide whether or not to have a barbecue.

If you roll an ordinary 1-6 dice there is a possibility that a 6 could end up on top. It might – or it might not.

If you're trying to find a way to work out a problem, you might get an idea that's worth thinking about. It might be worth trying – it's a possibility.

a b c d e f g h i j k l m n o Pp q r s t u v w x y z

pound

A pound can mean money or it can be a measure of weight in the imperial system.

Money: (£) pound

100 pence = £1.00 The decimal point separates the pounds from the pence. When pounds and pence are written down like this there are always two digits after the decimal point.

100p = £1.00	20p = £0.20 = £$\frac{1}{5}$
75p = £0.75 = £$\frac{3}{4}$	10p = £0.10 = £$\frac{1}{10}$
50p = £0.50 = £$\frac{1}{2}$	5p = £0.05 = £$\frac{1}{20}$
25p = £0.25 = £$\frac{1}{4}$	1p = £0.01 = £$\frac{1}{100}$

One pound fifty pence is written as £1.50
One pound five pence is written as £1.05

Weight: (lb) pound

The pound is also the name of a weight in the imperial system. These pounds are written as lb for short.
1 lb = 16 ounces.

1 lb weighs about 450 grams.
2·2 lbs weigh about 1 kilogram.

predict   prediction

If you predict something you say what you think will happen. You might predict the result of a football match or a science experiment. The weather forecast is a prediction of what the weather will be like.

prime factor

A factor is a whole number which will go exactly into another whole number, without leaving a remainder. A prime factor is a factor which is also a prime number. It can't be broken down into smaller equal groups.

3 is a prime factor of 21.   (21 ÷ 3 = 7)
7 is also a prime factor of 21. (21 ÷ 7 = 3)
Both will go into 21 an exact number of times and neither 3 nor 7 can be split into smaller equal groups.

10 is a factor of 20 but it is not a prime factor. 10 can be split into 2 x 5. The prime factors of 20 are 2, 2, and 5.   (2 x 2 x 5 = 20)
Look up **factor** and **prime numbers** if you want to know more about them.

prime numbers

Prime numbers are the awkward ones like 11, 17, 23, which don't break up into smaller equal groups.

You won't find them in the answers to your multiplication tables anywhere except when they are multiplied by 1.

They will only divide exactly by themselves and 1.
Examples of prime numbers are:
2, 3, 5, 7, 11, 13, 17, 19, 23, 29 ... ...

9 is not a prime number because it will split into three equal groups of three (3 x 3 = 9).

11 is a prime number because however you try to split it into equal groups, you have something left over. You can only have one group of eleven (1 x 11) or eleven ones (11 x 1).

1 is not counted as a prime number. It is a special case because 1 x 1 = 1.

prism

A prism is a special kind of 3D shape. Its two ends are the same size and shape and they are parallel to each other. A prism is the same size and shape all the way through its length. It doesn't get wider or narrower.

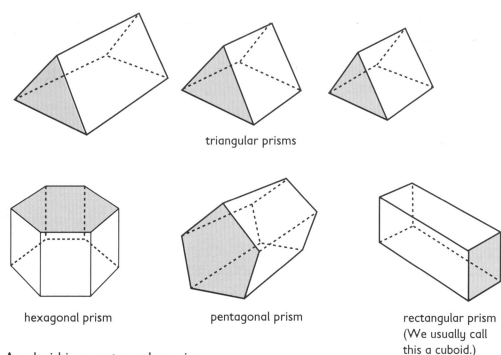

triangular prisms

hexagonal prism   pentagonal prism   rectangular prism
(We usually call
this a cuboid.)

A cuboid is a rectangular prism.
You may sometimes use triangular prisms in science lessons.

a
b
c
d
e
f
g
h
i
j
k
l
m
n
o
Pp
q
r
s
t
u
v
w
x
y
z

probability

If you roll a fair, six-sided 1-6 dice, what is the probability of it landing with the 6 on the top? We might say, *What's the chance of getting a 6?* or *How likely is it that you'll get a 6?* Probability is all about the likelihood of something happening – how likely it is to happen – what the chances are of it happening – how probable it is.

Suppose a bag had 2 blue blocks and 18 red ones in it. If you pulled one out without looking, you might get a blue one – it would be possible, but it would be unlikely. The probability of getting a red one would be much greater – that would be very likely.

If there were 10 blue blocks and 10 red ones there would be an equal chance of getting a red one or a blue one. There's an equal number of each. We might say that there was an even chance of getting either colour, or a fifty-fifty chance. You would be equally likely to get a red one or a blue one.

If **all** of the blocks were red you would be sure to get a red one – that would be certain. (You might say, 'That's a certainty!')

A dice like this has 6 faces with a different number on each one. When you roll the dice, only one of the 6 numbers has a chance of ending up on top. If it's a fair 1-6 dice you are equally likely to get a 1, 2, 3, 4, 5 or 6.
Your chance of getting a 6 is 1 out of the 6 possibilities. We could say that your chances are 1 out of 6.
We write that as $\frac{1}{6}$

When you roll the 1-6 dice, your chance of getting a 5 would be one out of 6, your chance of getting a 4 would be one out of 6 and so on.
There's no chance of getting a 7 – there's no 7 on the 1-6 dice so it would be impossible.

Look at this spinner. It has 8 edges.
The numbers on it are:

2 3 1 2 2 3 4 2

On this spinner there are more 2s than any other number – so you are more likely to get a 2 than any other number.
We could say that this spinner is **biased** in favour of 2s.

Out of the eight numbers, 4 of them are 2s. With one spin the probability of getting a 2 would be 4 out of 8.
(You could write $\frac{4}{8}$ or you could cancel $\frac{\cancel{4}^{1}}{\cancel{8}_{2}}$ to $\frac{1}{2}$.)

There are two 3s on this spinner so there would be 2 chances of getting a 3. The chances would be 2 out of 8.
(You could write $\frac{2}{8}$ or cancel it to $\frac{1}{4}$.)

There is only one 4 on this spinner, so the probability of getting a 4 is just 1 out of 8 ($\frac{1}{8}$). There is only one 1 on the spinner so you would have an equal chance of getting a 1. The chance of getting a 1 would be 1 out of 8 as well.

This is an example of a probability scale:

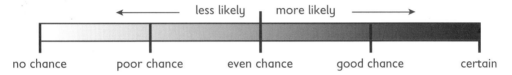

You might find it useful to look up **random**.

---

problems

If we call something a problem it sounds difficult before we start. That's a pity because it can make some people afraid to use their common sense. In maths some 'problems' mean working out everyday things, others are more like puzzles and some are a challenge for you. Often there is more than one way of working out a problem.

In this section there are some examples of different kinds of problems and some tips about tackling them.

Here are two problems to start with.

1 *Younis had 16 conkers. He found 4 more. Then he lost 1. How many did he have in the end?*

Take it step by step:
Younis had 16 + 4 = 20.
He lost 1.
He had 19 left.

2 *Jane bought some apples for £1.50 and some biscuits for 45p. How much did she spend altogether?*

She spent £1.50 + 45p.
Altogether she spent £1.95.

More ...

a
b
c
d
e
f
g
h
i
j
k
l
m
n
o
Pp
q
r
s
t
u
v
w
x
y
z

a
b
c
d
e
f
g
h
i
j
k
l
m
n
o
Pp
q
r
s
t
u
v
w
x
y
z

Now look at this one:
There are 6 picnic tables in a park.
If 5 people sit at each table, how many
people are there?

There are 6 tables.
5 people are at each table.

You could work out
    $5 + 5 + 5 + 5 + 5 + 5 = 30$ people
or $6 \times 5 = 30$ people.
There are 30 people there.

If you needed to you could draw 6 tables and 5 people at
each table. Then you could count them all up. It would take
you a lot longer but you could still get the right answer.

Some problems are more like puzzles. You can use an
empty box in the place of a number you don't know.
Look at this one:
If I multiply a certain number by 4, the answer is 12. What is
the answer if I multiply the same number by 5?

Read it, then take one step at a time.
The first sentence means
☐ (the number we don't know) x 4 = 12.
☐ x 4 = 12
 3 x 4 = 12
The 'certain number' must be 3.

Now look at the second sentence again:
What is the answer if I multiply the same number by 5?
$3 \times 5 = 15$
The answer is 15.

(Look up **number sentence** if you want to see some more
examples with missing numbers.)

Now what about this one?
If 5 bags cost £15, what is the cost of 2 bags?

This one is a different kind of problem and there are different ways of
working it out too. Some people call this way 'finding one first'.
If 5 bags cost £15 what is the cost of 2 bags?
First find the cost of 1 bag.
Then multiply by 2 to find the cost of 2 bags.

5 bags cost £15.
1 bag costs £15 ÷ 5 = £3.
2 bags cost £3 x 2 = £6.

Word problems:

When some people look at a maths problem written out in words they look at the words, and then they look at the numbers and wonder what to do with them. They don't give themselves a chance to get into the story.

Don't just look at the words. Read each sentence carefully. Think what you would do if you had to deal with this problem in real life. Sometimes underlining important words or drawing a diagram or a quick sketch will help you.

Read this problem:

A school was expecting 60 new books. The van delivered the books in 4 parcels. One contained 20 books, one contained 15 books and the other two contained 10 books each. How many were missing?

Now go back to the beginning.
They were expecting 60 books.
They got 20 + 15 + 10 + 10.
Altogether they got 55 books.
55 + 5 = 60
5 books were missing.

(Or you could take the number of books they **did** get away from 60 to find the missing number. 60 − 55 = 5, so 5 books were missing.)

Sometimes a problem seems difficult because you are not sure what some of the words mean or how they are used. Look them up.

A lot of the words you might need are in this book. There are reminders of how the words are used and examples of problems in many of the sections.

Remember:
1 Read carefully.
2 Underline the important information.
3 Then take it one step at a time.
Think: What do I need to find out?
What do I know?
What clues have I got?
4 If you need to, draw a quick diagram or sketch to help you see what it's all about.

a
b
c
d
e
f
g
h
i
j
k
l
m
n
o
Pp
q
r
s
t
u
v
w
x
y
z

product

In maths the product is the answer when something has been multiplied.

4 x 6 = 24

The product of 4 and 6 is 24.

profit

If we buy something for £2 and sell it for £3 we say we have made a profit of £1. The profit is the extra money. It is the amount we have gained.

properties

Your property is something you own. It is yours. Your property is something that belongs to you.

Some things in maths have properties. Their properties are things that they **always** have. These are properties of rectangles for example:

Rectangles have 4 sides and 4 angles.
The angles are all right angles.
The opposite sides are equal and they are parallel to each other.
Their diagonals bisect each other.

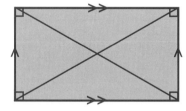

Look up **triangle** or **quadrilateral** to see some more examples of shapes and their properties.

proportion

We use proportion to compare things.
Look at these jam tarts. Altogether there are 10.
6 are blackcurrant and 4 are apricot.

6 out of the 10 are blackcurrant. ($\frac{6}{10}$ or $\frac{3}{5}$)

4 out of the 10 are apricot. ($\frac{4}{10}$ or $\frac{2}{5}$)

What proportion of them are blackcurrant ? $\frac{6}{10}$

What proportion of them are apricot? $\frac{4}{10}$

We could say that the proportion of blackcurrant tarts is 3 in every 5.
The proportion of apricot tarts is 2 in every 5.

Look at this string of beads. Some beads are red and some are white.

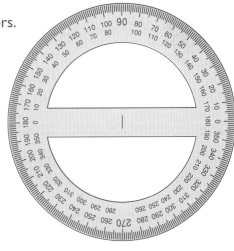

In every 4 beads there are 3 red ones and 1 white one.

The proportion of red beads is 3 in every 4. $\frac{3}{4}$ of the beads are red.

The proportion of white beads is 1 in every 4. $\frac{1}{4}$ of the beads are white.

Sometimes we might just say: The proportion of red beads is 3 in 4. The proportion of white beads is 1 in 4.

Here is another example of proportion:

Paul worked for 1 hour and Ali worked for 4 hours.
Share £20 between them in proportion to the number of hours
they worked.

Paul worked for 1 hour and Ali worked for 4 hours.
That makes 5 hours of work altogether.
£20 ÷ 5 = £4
There would be £4 for every hour they worked.

Paul worked for 1 hour out of the 5.
He would get 1 × £4.
Ali worked for 4 hours out of the 5.
He would get 4 × £4 = £16.

protractor

A protractor is used for drawing and measuring angles.
The sizes of the angles are measured in degrees.

Protractors can be circular or semi-circular. A semi-circular one is the sort we use most often.

There are two scales marked on protractors. One goes from left to right and the other starts at the right and comes back to the left. This means that we can measure angles facing either way.

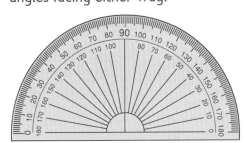

More ...

protractor

Measure the angle at B (ABC).

1 Find the base line on the protractor. (It will be marked 0° 180° at both ends.)

2 Put the middle of the base line exactly on the tip of the angle at B.

3 Let the left-hand end of the base line run along on top of the line CB.

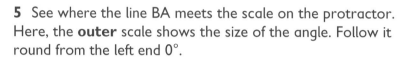

4 Hold the protractor still.

5 See where the line BA meets the scale on the protractor. Here, the **outer** scale shows the size of the angle. Follow it round from the left end 0°.

(As an angle is a measurement of turn we measure how far it has turned from 0°.)

Sometimes we have to make the arm of the angle a bit longer so that it reaches the scale on the protractor. This doesn't change the size of the angle. It doesn't open it any wider or close it up.

Measure the angle at E (DEF).

1 Find the base line again.

2 Put the middle of the base line exactly on the tip of the angle at E.

3 Let the right-hand side of the base line run along on top of the line EF.

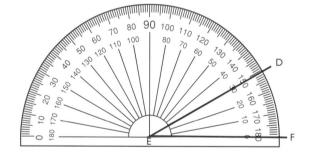

4 Hold the protractor still.

5 See where the line ED meets the scale on the protractor. Here the **inner** scale shows the size of the angle. (Follow it round from the right end 0°.)

If you are muddled by the two scales and don't know which answer is right, look at the size of your angle. See if it is more than a right angle (90°) or less. Then you should be able to choose the sensible answer.

Don't try to measure an angle upside down – turn your page round so that it is easy to manage.

Drawing an angle

If you have to draw an angle of a certain size you will need a protractor, a ruler and a pencil with a good point.

1 Draw a horizontal line to start with. Use a ruler to draw it and leave enough space above it for the rest of your angle to fit in.

2 Find the middle of the base line on your protractor and put it on one end of your line.

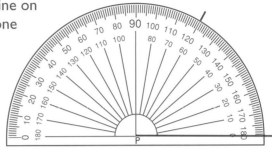

3 Look carefully round the scale from the 0° sign to the number you need for the size of your angle. (The example above shows 60°.) Put a dot on your page to mark where it comes to and then take the protractor away.

4 Rule a line from the point that was at the middle of your protractor (P in the diagram) through the mark you have just made.

5 Check the size of the angle you have drawn.

If you want to draw an angle facing the other way you start with the middle of your protractor at the other end of your line. Then look carefully round the scale from the 0° sign to the number you need for the size of your angle.

pyramid

A pyramid is a 3D shape. It has a flat base with straight sides – often a square or a triangle. The other faces are all triangles, they meet at a point at the top of the pyramid. This can be called the apex or vertex.

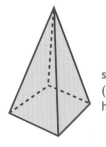

square pyramid
(a square pyramid
has a square base)

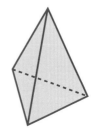

triangular pyramid
(a triangular pyramid
has a triangular base)

a
b
c
d
e
f
g
h
i
j
k
l
m
n
o
p

r
s
t
u
v
w
x
y
z

quadrant

A quadrant is a quarter of a circle.
Its angle (at the centre of the circle)
is a right angle.

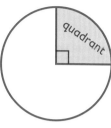

If you are dealing with **co-ordinates** you may use
the word quadrant like this:

Each quarter is a quadrant.

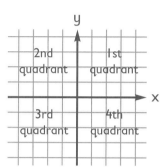

quadrilateral

A quadrilateral is a 2D shape with four straight sides.
The four angles inside it add up to 360° (degrees).
Some quadrilaterals have special names.

A square
A square has four equal sides. Each of its
angles is a right angle (90°). The opposite
sides are parallel.

A rectangle
Each angle of a rectangle is a right angle.
Its opposite sides are of equal length and
they are parallel to each other.
(A square is a special sort of rectangle
because all of its sides are equal.)

An oblong
Each angle of an oblong is a right angle. Its opposite sides
are parallel to each other and they are of equal length.
The sides which are next to each are not equal though.
An oblong is a rectangle but it is never a square.

A parallelogram
A parallelogram has two pairs of
parallel sides. Its opposite sides
are equal in length.

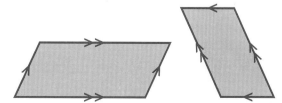

A rhombus
A rhombus has four equal sides.
The opposite sides are parallel.

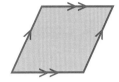

A trapezium
A trapezium is a quadrilateral which
has a pair of parallel sides.

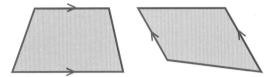

A kite
A kite has two pairs of adjacent sides
which are equal in length. One pair
is longer than the other. (Adjacent
means next to each other.)

quarter

If something is divided into four equal pieces or groups, each
part is called a quarter.

It can be written as $\frac{1}{4}$ (1 out of the 4)

two quarters $= \frac{2}{4}$ or $\frac{1}{2}$

three quarters $= \frac{3}{4}$

four quarters make up a whole one. $\frac{1}{4} + \frac{1}{4} + \frac{1}{4} + \frac{1}{4} = 1$

To find a quarter of something we divide it by 4. We can
also do this by halving and halving again.

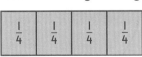

Two quarters = a half. $\frac{1}{4} + \frac{1}{4} = \frac{1}{2}$

Three quarters is written $\frac{3}{4}$ $\frac{1}{4} + \frac{1}{4} + \frac{1}{4} = \frac{3}{4}$

A quarter of an hour ($\frac{1}{4}$ hr) is 15 minutes.

To quarter something is to cut it – or divide it – into four equal parts.

quotient

(Say 'kwo-shnt'.) The quotient is the number of times one number can be divided into another. It is the answer to a division calculation.

$10 \div 5 = 2$
The quotient is 2.

$11 \div 5 = 2$ remainder 1
We can write 2rem1 or 2r1.

11 pencils divided between 5 people would mean that they could have 2 each and 1 pencil would be left over.

The remainder can be shown in different ways. Sometimes it's something that is left over – like the pencil – and we write it down like the example above.
Often it is part of something and we take the division one step further. We divide the bit that is left over as well.

> Remember:
> $1 \div 2 = \frac{1}{2}$
> $1 \div 3 = \frac{1}{3}$
> $2 \div 3 = \frac{2}{3}$
> $1 \div 4 = \frac{1}{4}$
> $3 \div 4 = \frac{3}{4}$ and so on.

$12 \div 2 = 6$ $13 \div 2 = 6\frac{1}{2}$

$10 \div 3 = 3\frac{1}{3}$ $11 \div 3 = 3\frac{2}{3}$ $12 \div 3 = 4$

$7 \div 4 = 1\frac{3}{4}$ $28 \div 5 = 5\frac{3}{5}$ $7 \div 5 = 1\frac{2}{5}$ $15 \div 10 = 1\frac{5}{10} = 1\frac{1}{2}$

Sometimes we need to give the answer as a decimal:

$15 \div 10 = 1 \cdot 5$ $13 \div 2 = 6 \cdot 5$

$17 \div 10 = 1 \cdot 7$ $13 \div 4 = 3 \cdot 25$

$17 \div 100 = 0 \cdot 17$ $19 \div 4 = 4 \cdot 75$

radius radii *(The plural of radius is radii.)*

(Say 'raydee-i'.) The radius of a circle is the distance from the centre of the circle to its circumference (the curved edge). All radii of the same circle are equal in length.

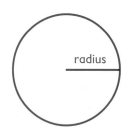

To draw a circle with a radius of – say – 3cm, the point of your pencil and the point of your compasses must be exactly 3cm apart.

There is some more information which might be useful to you in the sections on **compasses** and **circle**.

random

If you dipped your hand into a bag of marbles and took one out without looking, we would say that you had picked one out at random. You didn't choose that particular one – you got it by chance. You could have got any one of those marbles.

range

The range of a list of numbers tells you how far the list spreads.

To find the range we find the difference between the highest number and the lowest number in the list. Look at this list:
3 8 6 2 6 15 12

The highest number is 15. The lowest number is 2.
15 – 2 = 13 The range is 13.

ratio

(Say 'ray-she-o'.) One way of comparing things is to write them down as a ratio.

Look at these 5 animals.
There are 3 cats and 2 dogs.
We could say that the ratio
of **cats to dogs** is **3 to 2**.

Suppose there were 3 vehicles in a garage.
If 2 were cars and 1 was a motor-bike we could say that there were twice as many cars as motor-bikes.
We could also say that the ratio of **cars to motor-bikes** was **2 to 1**.

Looking at it the other way we could say there were half as many motor-bikes as cars.
We could say that the ratio of **motor-bikes to cars** was **1 to 2**.

More ...

Sometimes we are dealing with larger numbers.
Suppose there were 40 vehicles altogether in a car park:
10 vans and 30 cars. The ratio of vans to cars was 10 to 30.
We could say that for every van there were 3 cars.

We usually write a ratio as simply as we can, using the
lowest whole numbers possible. We could say that the ratio
of vans to cars was 1 to 3. This might be written 1:3.

(The **proportion** of vans in the car park would be 10 out of
the 40 vehicles. 1 in every 4 or $\frac{1}{4}$ of them. The proportion of
cars in the car park would be 30 out of the 40 vehicles. 3 in
every 4 or $\frac{3}{4}$ of them.

Look up **proportion** if you want to know more about that.)

rectangle

A rectangle is a 2D shape with 4 sides.
Its angles are all right angles.
Its opposite sides are equal and they are parallel to each other.

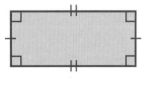
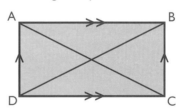

The diagonals of a rectangle are equal.
(Look at the diagram. AC = BD)
The diagonals bisect one another.

To find the perimeter of a rectangle, add up the length of all
its sides.

To find the area of a rectangle, multiply its length by its
breadth (width). (Don't forget, this answer will be a square
measure – a number of mm^2 or cm^2 or m^2 for example.)

Look up **perimeter** or **area** if you need to know more.
(A square is a special kind of rectangle.)

recur recurring

If something recurs, it happens again. It is repeated.

A recurring decimal is a decimal fraction which can never be worked out exactly: a digit or a pattern of digits is repeated over and over again.

$\frac{1}{3}$ is an example of this. If it is changed to a decimal fraction

$\frac{1}{3}$ comes to 0·33333333 … and it would go on and on forever …!

Instead of writing lots of 3s we put a little dot in the air over the last digit, like this: 0·$\dot{3}$ or 0·3$\dot{3}$ (We say, 'point three recurring' or 'point three three recurring' and so on.)
The little dot above the number shows that it is a recurring decimal.

If it is a recurring pattern of digits we put a little dot above the first and last digits of the pattern.

19 ÷ 11 = 1·727272 and so on.

We could write 19 ÷ 11 = 1·$\dot{7}\dot{2}$

12 ÷ 7 = 1·$\dot{7}$1428$\dot{5}$714

reduce reduction

To reduce something is to make it less or smaller. If the price of something is reduced it is made lower. It costs less. If we reduce our weight we lose some weight. We weigh less.

If the price of a £5 book was reduced by £1 we would pay £4 for it. £1 would be taken off its price.

If the usual price of something is £1.50 and the sale price is £1 the reduction is 50p. (It's the difference between the two prices.)
If something is reduced by 5%, $\frac{5}{100}$ of the price is taken off.

(Look up **percentages** if you need to know more about this.)

Reduce to its lowest terms means bring down to the lowest numbers you can.

$\frac{5}{10}$ reduced to its lowest terms is $\frac{1}{2}$ but the fraction is still worth the

same. $\frac{5}{10} = \frac{1}{2}$ $\frac{8}{4}$ reduced to its lowest terms is 2. $\frac{8}{4} = 2$

reflection

If you look in a mirror you see a reflection. If you hold a mirror at different angles or different heights you will see different reflections.

If you touch the mirror you don't feel what you see, you just feel the mirror. What you see is called a reflection of the real thing.

a b c d e f g h i j k l m n o p r **Rr** s t u v w x y z

a
b
c
d
e
f
g
h
i
j
k
l
m
n
o
p
q

Rr

s
t
u
v
w
x
y
z

reflective symmetry

If a shape can be divided into two matching halves we say it has reflective symmetry. One half reflects – or 'mirrors' – the other. Reflective symmetry is sometimes called line symmetry.

Look at these examples:

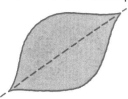 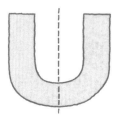  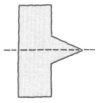

The dividing line is called the **line of symmetry** or the **mirror line** (It is also sometimes called the **axis of symmetry**.)

If a shape that has reflective symmetry is cut out and folded along a line of symmetry, or mirror line, one side will fit exactly on top of the other.

Some shapes don't have a line of symmetry. Some have more than one.

The letter H could be divided like this Both halves would match either way. It has 2 lines of symmetry.   or like this.

A square has 4 lines of symmetry.

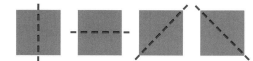

Sometimes you may need to draw the reflection of a shape as it would look in a mirror. Look at this example:

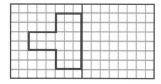 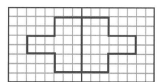

If you are working on a grid or paper with dots on, you can count the squares or the dots to help you do this. Sometimes you may use tracing paper to help you.
If you're not sure about it practise this when you have some spare time.

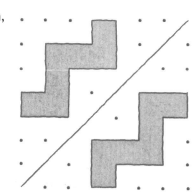

Sometimes you might need to draw the reflection of a **whole** shape in a mirror line, like this:

(Look up **mirror line** if you aren't sure about it.)

reflex angle

Reflex angles measure between 180° and 360°.
These angles are so wide open that they look as if their sides have been bent backwards.

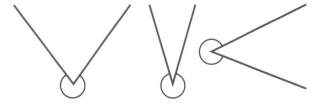

Look up **angles** if you want to know more about them.

regular shapes

A regular shape has all of its sides and all of its angles equal.
(The sections under **polygon** or **polyhedron** might interest you.)

relations   relationship

Relations are connected to each other in some way. There is a relationship between them.

There is a relationship between 2 and 4:
2 is half of 4.   4 is twice 2.

There is a relationship between centimetres and metres.

$100cm = 1$ metre $1cm = \frac{1}{100}$ metre

If you have to find the relationship between two or more things, you have to find out how they are connected.

In a list of numbers there may be a relationship between one number and the next, for example, 5 10 15 20 25. The numbers are going up in size and each number is 5 bigger than the one before it.
(The section under **sequence** gives you more examples about this.)

It might help you to look up **ratio** or **proportion** if you have been dealing with either of those.

remainder

A remainder is something that is left over.

$6 \div 2 = 3$

$7 \div 2 = 3$ remainder 1
(We can write 3rem1 or 3r1)

$11 \div 4 = 2r3$

Sometimes we need to show the remainder as a fraction or a decimal.
Look up **quotient** if you need to know about that.

a
b
c
d
e
f
g
h
i
j
k
l
m
n
o
p
q
Rr
s
t
u
v
w
x
y
z

a
b
c
d
e
f
g
h
i
j
k
l
m
n
o
p
q
Rr
s
t
u
v
w
x
y
z

repeat

If you repeat something you say it – or do it – again.
If something is repeated it is said – or done – again.

Sometimes a pattern may be repeated over and over again.
This is often called a repeating pattern.
Here are some examples.

A pattern of numbers is sometimes repeated in maths. You
might be interested to look up **recur**.

represents

Represents means 'stands for' or 'stands in place of'.
In maths we often use signs or symbols to represent words.

> represents 'is more than'.   We could write 6 > 5.
< represents 'is less than'.   We could write 5 < 6.

Sometimes a letter is used to represent a number that we
don't know. It stands in the place where the number should
be until we have worked out what it is.

On a pictogram one symbol often represents a larger
number of people or things.
(Look up **graphs** if you want to see an example of this.
A pictogram is right near the beginning.)

On maps and plans symbols often represent things of special
interest. (There is an example of this under **plan**.)

When things are drawn to scale, 1 cm might represent a
much greater length.
(Look up **scale** if you want to know more about that.)

revolution

In maths a revolution is a complete turn. A bicycle wheel
makes one revolution every time it goes round.

rhombus

A rhombus is 2D shape. It has four
sides that are all equal in length.
The opposite sides are parallel.

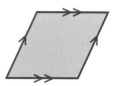

right angle

Angles of 90° are called right angles. (They are often marked on diagrams by a tiny square.)

To make a useful right angle, fold any scrap of paper into four like this:

Make sure the edges of the folds are level.
Then you have a right angle which you can use for checking the size of any other angles. (You can see if they are also right angles, or if they are greater or smaller than a right angle.)
Look up **angles** if you want more information about them.

right-angled triangle

A right-angled triangle has an angle that measures 90°.
(90° is a right angle.)

On diagrams right angles are often marked with a tiny square.

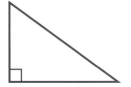  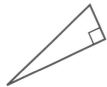

ring pictures

Ring pictures help to sort out groups – or sets – of things.

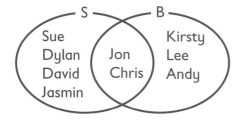

S is a group of people who go swimming.
B is a group of people who play in a band.
Jon and Chris are in both rings.
They go swimming **and** they play in a band so the rings overlap.

Ring pictures are usually called **Venn diagrams** in maths.

a
b
c
d
e
f
g
h
i
j
k
l
m
n
o
p
q
Rr
s
t
u
v
w
x
y
z

rotate rotation

If something rotates it turns round. If you rotate something you turn it round. A complete rotation is a whole turn, right the way round. A whole turn is 360°. (This is equal to 4 right angles.)

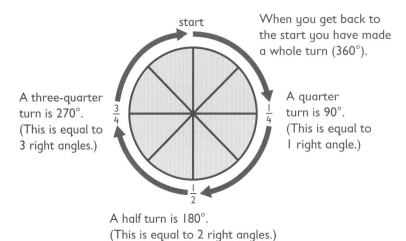

start

When you get back to the start you have made a whole turn (360°).

A three-quarter turn is 270°. (This is equal to 3 right angles.)

A quarter turn is 90°. (This is equal to 1 right angle.)

A half turn is 180°. (This is equal to 2 right angles.)

When something rotates it turns around a central point. It doesn't move away.

round numbers

Sometimes we don't need to know an exact number of something: a rough idea is good enough. 'Round numbers' are often easier to deal with and easier to remember than exact numbers. Round numbers usually end in a zero or a number of zeros.

'Round numbers' are a kind of **approximation**. The next section about **rounding** numbers may help you too.

rounding

By rounding numbers we can find approximate answers. This is useful when we need a rough answer. It is also useful when we want to estimate a result or check our working out. It shows us if we have got a sensible answer or if we are a long way out.

Rounding to the nearest ten
When we round to the nearest ten, we don't use any units. We round the number up to the ten above it or down to the ten below it, whichever is nearer.

24 would be rounded down to 20.   27 would be rounded up to 30.

146 would be rounded up to 150.   1242 would be rounded down to 1240.

If you have a number ending in 5 it is half-way between two tens. Round it up to the higher ten. 45 would be rounded up to 50.

Rounding to the nearest hundred

When we round a number to the nearest hundred, we don't
use any tens or units. We round the number to the hundred
above it or the hundred below it, whichever is the nearer.

140 would be rounded down to 100.   162 would be rounded up to 200.
1449 would be rounded down to 1400.

If you have a number ending in 50 it is half-way between two hundreds.
Round it up to the hundred above it. 1250 would be rounded up to 1300.

Rounding to the nearest thousand

When we round numbers to the nearest thousand, we don't
use any hundreds, tens or units. We round the number to the
thousand above it or the thousand below it, whichever is nearer.

1427 would be rounded down to 1000.   1538 would be rounded up to 2000.
15960 would be rounded up to 16000.

If you have a number ending exactly in 500 it is half-way
between two thousands. Round it up to the thousand above it.
14500 would be rounded up to 15000.

Rounding to the nearest whole number

Sometimes we need to round up or down to the nearest
whole number. If we are dealing with fractions or decimals:

$1\frac{7}{8}$ would be rounded up to 2. $1\frac{3}{8}$ would be rounded down to 1.

2·75 would be rounded up to 3.   2·25 would be rounded down to 2.

Rounding to a number of decimal places

We sometimes have to round a decimal up or down so that
it is 'correct to a certain number of decimal places.'
3·714 correct to 2 decimal places would be 3·71
3·718 correct to 2 decimal places would be 3·72

Rounding up or down?

When you are rounding a number you sometimes have to use
your common sense about whether you round it up or down.
Look at this example:
Some minibuses take up to 12 people each.
How many would you need to order for 28 people?

28 ÷ 12 = 2r4

It would be no good rounding that down to 2.
If you only ordered 2 minibuses 4 people
would be left behind! You would have to
round it up to 3 and order 3 minibuses.

scale

1 In maths the word scale has something to do with weighing or measuring. The marks on a ruler are a kind of scale: they help us to draw lines of a certain length – or to measure lines to see how long they are.

We use a scale on a protractor to measure angles in degrees.

A scale is marked on a thermometer so that we can see what the temperature is. (Look up **Celsius** if you want to know about the Celsius scale.)

We may use kitchen scales when we are cooking. If we need 350 grams of flour, for example, we put some flour on the scale pan a bit at a time and watch the scale until the pointer reaches 350g. Then we know we have the right amount.

(If it goes past the 350g we have too much flour – we have to take a bit off and adjust it until we get the right amount.)

This shows 350g.
Some scales are marked in kilograms (kg).
1000g = 1 kg
350g = 0·35kg

2 Drawing or building to scale

We may also talk about something being '**to scale**'.

A model may be built to scale. You may have a kit for making a scale model of a plane or a famous building. Set designers make scale models of the sets they will use for television programmes or stage plays. If a model is built to scale every part of it is carefully measured and made smaller in the same way.

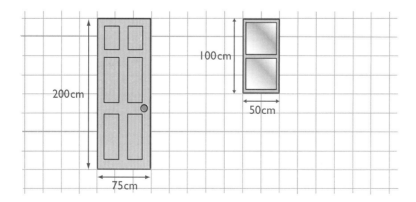

A diagram or a map or plan may be drawn to scale. Usually a plan can't be drawn life-size. It has to fit on to a piece of paper. If it is drawn to scale everything is carefully measured and made smaller in the same way.

If something which is 1 metre long is drawn as 1 centimetre long, we would say that 1 centimetre represents 1 metre. On that scale something which measures 2 metres in real life would be drawn 2 centimetres long.

Something measuring $\frac{1}{2}$ metre in real life would measure $\frac{1}{2}$ centimetre on the plan.

A scale of 1:20 (we say 1 to 20) means that each measurement is $\frac{1}{20}$ of the real life measurement.

1cm would stand for 20cm.
2cm would stand for 40cm.
The real-life measurements would be 20 x the measurements on the plan or model.

If you are comparing different diagrams or plans remember to look at the scales they are drawn to. If the scales are different it's very difficult to compare them. You may need to work out or estimate the real-life sizes.

Look up **plan** for some more information that might interest you.

scalene triangle

A scalene triangle has no equal sides and no equal angles.

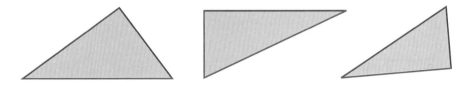

There is a section about **triangles** if you want to know more about them – there is another scalene triangle there as well.

score

A score can be a number of points you have won in a game – or the number of goals or runs a team has scored.

If you are **keeping a score** you make a list of the people's names and then jot down the points as they are won. At the end of the game you add up the points to get the results. Those results will be the **final score**.

A score is also an old-fashioned name for twenty. Three score years and ten means 70. (Three twenties plus ten.)

seasons

The seasons of the year are spring, summer, autumn and winter.

a
b
c
d
e
f
g
h
i
j
k
l
m
n
o
p
q
r
Ss
t
u
v
w
x
y
z

second

1 A second is a **measure of time**.

60 seconds = 1 minute	30 seconds = $\frac{1}{2}$ minute
15 seconds = $\frac{1}{4}$ minute	45 seconds = $\frac{3}{4}$ minute

There is more information in the section on **time**.

2 This word can also be used another way. Second can mean **next after the first one**.
The person who wins a race comes first (1st). The next person to finish comes second (2nd). The one after that comes third (3rd).

You might eat a second cake after you've finished your first one.

select

If you select something you choose it – you pick it out.

semi-circle

A semi-circle is half of a circle.

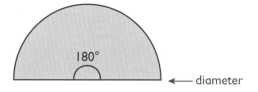

180°

← diameter

separate

If you separate things you move them away from each other – you move them apart.

If you were sorting out some numbers you might separate the odd ones from the even ones. You could put them into two separate lists.

sequence

In maths we might talk about a sequence of events or a number sequence. In a sequence, things follow on one after another.

This is a sequence of even numbers:
2   4   6   8   10   12   14   16 . . . .

Sometimes we need to find **missing numbers in a sequence**.

Look at the numbers you are given. If you can see a pattern in the sequence you can carry on with that pattern to find the missing numbers.

If you can't see a pattern or a rule, see if the numbers are getting bigger or smaller. See how you can get from one number to the next. Look at this example. There are two missing numbers at the end:

20   17   14   11   ☐   ☐

20 − 3 = 17   17 − 3 = 14   14 − 3 = 11

so carry on   11 − 3 = 8   8 − 3 = 5

3 is being taken away each time. The missing numbers are **8** and **5**.

If the numbers in the list are getting bigger something may be added on to them or they may be multiplied by something. If the numbers are getting smaller, something may be subtracted (taken away) from them or they may be divided by something.

Missing numbers aren't always at the end of the list:

6   11   16   ☐   26   31   ☐   41

Here 5 is added on to each number to get to the next.

16 + 5 = 21   The first missing number is **21**

31 + 5 = 36   The second missing number is **36**

This list doesn't go up in equal steps:

4   6   9   13   18   ☐   ☐

See how you get from each number to the next.

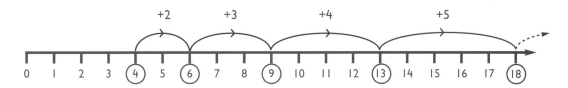

Carry on using the same pattern (or rule) to put in the next two numbers:

18 + 6 = 24   24 + 7 = 31

You may find it interesting to look up **square numbers** and **triangular numbers**. The diagrams show how those sequences are built up.

The sequence of square numbers starts:

1   4   9   16   25 . . . .

The sequence of triangular numbers starts:

1   3   6   10   15   21 . . . .

a
b
c
d
e
f
g
h
i
j
k
l
m
n
o
p
q
r
Ss
t
u
v
w
x
y
z

a
b
c
d
e
f
g
h
i
j
k
l
m
n
o
p
q
r
Ss
t
u
v
w
x
y
z

set square

A set square is used for drawing parallel lines and perpendicular lines. It is shaped like a triangle. One of its angles is a right angle. It would fit the corner of a square. Sometimes the other two angles on a set square are equal and measure 45° each. Sometimes the other angles measure 60° and 30°.

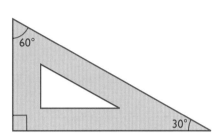
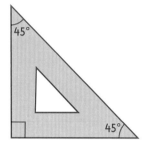

A set square can be useful for measuring these angles.

By sliding the bottom edge of a set square along a straight line we can rule parallel lines. You may find it better to put a ruler beside the set square and rule the lines along that. If you've got a bit of spare time, try it and see.

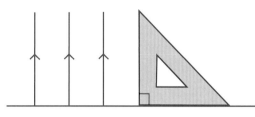

These vertical lines are parallel to each other and they are also perpendicular to the base line. Look up **perpendicular** and **parallel lines** if you have forgotten about them.

share sharing

When we talk about sharing we usually mean sharing equally. We can share things like this by dividing them up into equal groups or pieces.
÷ is the sign for division.

If you share 10 sweets equally between 2 children they would have 5 sweets each.
10 ÷ 2 = 5.
If you want to know more about this kind of sharing look up **division**.

Sometimes you may have to share things out differently so that one person has a certain amount more than another – or because one thing costs a certain amount more than another.
If you need to know about that, look up **unequal sharing**.

signs and symbols

Signs and symbols save a lot of time – and space. We use them to stand in place of words that we often need to use. Sometimes they can stand in a place where there isn't room to write out the words in full. This list of signs and symbols and their meanings includes those you are most likely to need in maths.

+ add, plus. This is the addition sign. (+ is sometimes put in front of a number to show that it is positive.)

− take away, subtract, minus. This is the subtraction sign (− is also put before a number that is negative.)

× multiply, multiplied by, times. This is the multiplication sign.

÷ divided by, shared between. This is the division sign.

= equals, is equal to, makes, is worth the same as. This is the equals sign.

≠ is not equal to.

≈ approximately, approximately equal to, about, roughly.

> is greater than, more than, bigger than, larger than.

< is less than, fewer than, smaller than.
  (Think of > as a hungry mouth. It always opens towards the bigger amount. 3 < 10 means 3 is less than 10. 10 > 3 means 10 is greater than 3.)

≥ is greater than or equal to. 5 ≥ ☐ means that 5 is either greater than the number missing from the box or equal to it.

≤ is less than or equal to. 5 ≤ ☐ means that 5 is either less than the number missing from the box or equal to it.

£ This is the pound sign (for money).

% per cent, out of every hundred, in every hundred. This is the percentage sign.

° degree or degrees. °C degrees Celsius. °F degrees Fahrenheit.

∠ angle

△ triangle

☐ square

// parallel to

⊥ perpendicular to

√ the square root of

Little arrowheads on lines tell us that they are parallel lines.

Little dashes on lines show us that they are equal in length.

A little square drawn in an angle tells us that it is a right angle (90°).

Symbols are also used on maps and plans where there isn't much space for writing words. A separate list, often called a 'key,' tells people what those symbols stand for. Look up **plan** if you want to see an example of this. Symbols may also be used on charts and **pictograms**.

a
b
c
d
e
f
g
h
i
j
k
l
m
n
o
p
q
r
Ss
t
u
v
w
x
y
z

a
b
c
d
e
f
g
h
i
j
k
l
m
n
o
p
q
r
Ss
t
u
v
w
x
y
z

simplify

If we simplify something we make it as easy to deal with as possible.

To simplify a fraction we bring it down to its lowest terms.

$$\frac{10}{100} = \frac{1}{10} \qquad \frac{3}{2} = 1\frac{1}{2} \qquad \frac{13}{2} = 6\frac{1}{2}$$

$$\frac{\cancel{10}^{2}}{\cancel{15}_{3}} = \frac{2}{3}$$

Look up **fractions** if you have forgotten about this.

To simplify an expression, a number sentence or an equation, we work it out and put the answer as simply as we can. Sometimes there is more than one way to do it.

$4 + 10 - 8\ = 14 - 8 = 6$ OR

$4 + (10 - 8) =\ 4 + 2 = 6$

The answer is 6.

$n + 7 = 10$
$3 + 7 = 10$
$n = 3$

solid figures solids

Three-dimensional (3D) shapes are not flat shapes like squares and circles – they have length and breadth (width) and height. 3D shapes may be solid or hollow.
If they are solid they are sometimes called **solid figures** or **solids**.

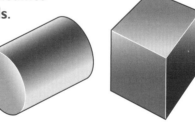

Look up **three-dimensional (3D)** shapes if you want to see some more examples of them.

solution solve

If you have to find a solution to a problem – or solve a problem – you have to find an answer to it. You need to think about it carefully and work it out.
(The section on **problems** might help you. There are examples of solving problems in a lot of other places in this book as well.)

speed

Speed is how fast someone or something moves. Another word for speed is velocity.
Speed is often measured in **kilometres per hour** (km/h) or **miles per hour** (mph).

If you cycle steadily at 16km/h you go 16 kilometres in every hour.

In 2 hours you would travel 2 x 16 km (32km).

In 3 hours you would travel 3 x 16 km (48km).

In $\frac{1}{2}$ hour you would travel $\frac{1}{2}$ of 16 km (8km).

If you cycle steadily at 10 mph (miles per hour) you go 10 miles in every hour.

In $\frac{1}{2}$ hour you would travel $\frac{1}{2}$ of 10 miles (5 miles).

In 2 hours you would travel 2 x 10 miles (20 miles).

It is very difficult to cycle at exactly the same speed all the time even if there are no hills or traffic. When people talk about speed they usually mean **average** speed.
A man might drive a car at an average speed of 40 mph on a journey. Sometimes he might drive more slowly, sometimes he might drive more quickly, but if his speed were divided out evenly over the whole journey it would come to 40 mph. That was his average speed.

To find the speed of something — or the average speed — we divide the **total distance** (the number of miles or kilometres) by the **total amount of time** taken (the number of hours or fractions of an hour). The answer will be a number of miles per hour (mph) or kilometres per hour (km/h).

There is a formula for this:

Speed (in mph) = distance (in miles)   ÷ time (in hours)
Speed (in km/h) = distance (in km)   ÷ time (in hours)

If a girl cycles for 32 km and takes 2 hours to do it, her average speed is 16 km/h (32 ÷ 2 = 16).

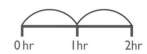
0 hr   1 hr   2hr

If a man drives for 200 miles and takes 4 hours to do it, his average speed is 50 mph (200 ÷ 4 = 50).

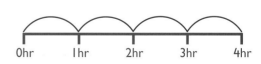
0hr   1hr   2hr   3hr   4hr

You might find it helpful to look up **distance** and **time**.

sphere

(Say 'sfeer'.) A sphere is a 3D shape that is round in every direction. It is like a round ball.

spherical

(Say 'sferrical'.) Something which is spherical is shaped like a sphere.

square

1 A square is a 2D shape.
It has 4 straight sides. They are all of equal length.
It has 4 angles and they are all right angles (90°).
The opposite sides are parallel.

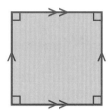

A square has 4 lines of symmetry.

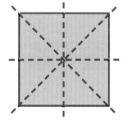

2 A square number
To square a number we multiply it by itself. The answer is called a square number.
3 x 3 = 9
9 is a square number.

If you want to know more about this look at the next section: **square numbers**. You may want to look up **squared** as well.

square numbers

When a number has been multiplied by itself we call it a square number. (If you look at the diagrams you will see why!)

   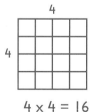

| 1 x 1 = 1 | 2 x 2 = 4 | 3 x 3 = 9 | 4 x 4 = 16 |

1, 4, 9, 16 are all square numbers

The next square numbers are:

25 (5 x 5) **36** (6 x 6) **49** (7 x 7) **64** (8 x 8)

81 (9 x 9) **100** (10 x 10) **121** (11 x 11) **144** (12 x 12) and so on.

square root

$\sqrt{\ }$ You can see this sign on a calculator. It's the square root sign.
$\sqrt{16}$ means the square root of 16.
A square root is the opposite of a square number.

$3 \times 3 = 9$	The square root of 9 is 3.	$\sqrt{9} = 3$
$4 \times 4 = 16$	The square root of 16 is 4.	$\sqrt{16} = 4$
$5 \times 5 = 25$	The square root of 25 is 5.	$\sqrt{25} = 5$
$10 \times 10 = 100$	The square root of 100 is 10	$\sqrt{100} = 10$

squared

A number which is squared is multiplied by itself.

4 squared is written as 4^2
It means 4×4
$4^2 = 16$

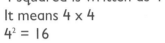

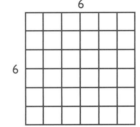

6 squared is written as 6^2
It means 6×6
$6^2 = 36$

10 squared is written as 10^2
It means 10×10
$10^2 = 100$

1 squared is written as 1^2
It means 1×1
$1^2 = 1$

statistics

Statistics are collections of facts and figures.

straight angle

An angle of 180° is a straight angle.

strategy

If you have a problem you might work out a strategy to
solve it. A strategy is a kind of plan.

subtraction

Subtraction is 'taking away'. The answer is the number which is left.

Here are four sweets.
If we subtract 1, we take away 1.
3 are left.

The sign we use for subtraction is **—**. It is called the minus sign.
4 – 1 = 3.

We use subtraction for all the following examples.

From 5 *take away* 2

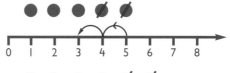

5 – 2 = 3

From 6 *subtract* 2

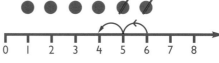

6 – 2 = 4

8 *minus* 3

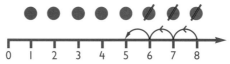

8 – 3 = 5

Decrease 4 by 3

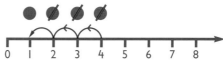

4 – 3 = 1

Reduce 7 by 4

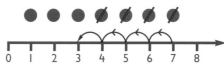

7 – 4 = 3

Take 6 from 10. You must write down the 10 first so that
you can take 6 away from it.

Take 6 from 10 means 10 – 6.   10 – 6 = 4
Subtract 4 from 5 means 5 – 4.   5 – 4 = 1
Deduct 5 from 7 means 7 – 5.   7 – 5 = 2

4 *less than* 6

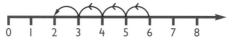

6 – 4 = 2

*By how much is 6 less
than 8?*

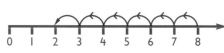

8 – 6 = 2

*Which number is 4 fewer
than 7?*

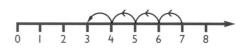

7 – 4 = 3

How many is 4 less than 5?

5 – 4 = 1

When we find the difference between the two amounts we have to compare them.
What is the difference between 6 and 4?

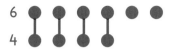

6 is 2 more than 4. The difference between 6 and 4 is 2.
6 – 4 = 2
(There is more about this under **difference** if you need it.)

surface

If you put your hand flat on the top of your table and slide it along, you are feeling the surface of the table.
When you touch things you might feel a smooth surface or a rough surface, a hard surface or a soft surface. On a freezing cold day the roads might have a slippery surface.

The surface is the outer layer of something. It has length and breadth (width) or height and breadth – but it doesn't have any depth.

surface area

Read **surface** first if you aren't quite sure about it – it comes just before this section.

To find the surface area of something we find the areas of its faces and add them all together. (Remember, the areas will be **square** measures, a number of cm^2 for example.)

Look at the faces of this **cuboid**.

The top	=10cm x 6cm	= $60cm^2$
The base	=10cm x 6cm	= $60cm^2$
1st long side	=10cm x 3cm	= $30cm^2$
2nd long side	=10cm x 3cm	= $30cm^2$
1st short side	= 3cm x 6cm	= $18cm^2$
2nd short side	= 3cm x 6cm	= $18cm^2$

6cm
3cm
10cm

Add together the areas of each face to find the total surface area of the cuboid. The answer is 216 cm^2
(In this example you could add 2 lots of 60 cm^2 + 2 lots of 30 cm^2 + 2 lots of 18 cm^2. That's (120 + 60 + 36) cm^2 which comes to 216 cm^2).

symbols

We use symbols to save time and space. They often stand for words that we use a lot – but you do need to know what they stand for. There's a list of symbols that are often used in maths under **signs and symbols**. It also tells you what they mean.

symmetrical

If both halves of a shape match each other as if they are seen in a mirror, we say that the shape is symmetrical. These shapes are both symmetrical.

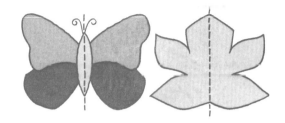

symmetry

The diagrams under **symmetrical** both show symmetry. You can divide each of them into matching halves that 'mirror' each other. This kind of symmetry is called **reflective symmetry**.
The dividing line is called the **line of symmetry**, **the mirror line**, or the **axis of symmetry**. Some shapes have more than one line of symmetry.

The letter H could be divided like this. Both halves would match either way. It has two lines (or **axes**) of symmetry. These are also called mirror lines.

or like this.

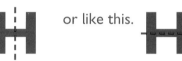

A square has four lines (or axes) of symmetry.

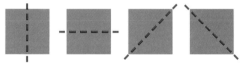

If a symmetrical shape is cut out and folded along the line of symmetry, one side will fit exactly on top of the other.

Some shapes don't have a line of symmetry at all.

If you want to know more about this there are sections on **mirror line**, **reflection** and **reflective symmetry** which should help you.

Rotational Symmetry
Rotational symmetry is another sort of symmetry. Remember, a complete **rotation** is a whole turn, right the way round. Rotational symmetry is about turning shapes to see how many times they match their own outline in a complete rotation.
This shape is an equilateral triangle. Imagine there is a pin through the dot in the middle to hold it in place. Think of the shape rotating.

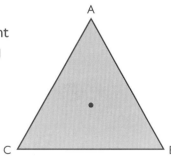

1 It will match its own shape exactly when A is in B's place.
2 It will match it again when A is in C's place.
3 It will match it again when A is back at A's place.
It matches its own shape 3 times in a complete turn. This is called rotational symmetry to the order of 3.
The centre point (where the dot is) is called the centre of **rotation**.

tables

When information is arranged in a list it is often called a table. A table of information can also be arranged in columns – or in rows and columns. We talk about tables of measurements, multiplication tables, a table of results, timetables and so on. (Look up **timetable** if you want to know more about these.)

A multiplication table is a list of equal groups already counted up. Read the section on **multiplication** if you want to know how they are built up and what they mean.

This table shows the numbers of children there are in each class of a school.

class	number of children
1	27
2	25
3	32
4	30
5	29
6	31

Metric units

Length
10 millimetres (mm) = 1 centimetre (cm)
100 centimetres = 1 metre (m)
1000 metres = 1 kilometre (km)

Area (square measure)
100 mm^2 = 1 cm^2
10 000 cm^2 = 1 m^2

Mass (or weight)
1000 milligrams (mg) = 1 gram (g)
1000 grams = 1 kilogram (kg)
1000 kilograms = 1 tonne

Capacity
1000 millilitres (ml) = 1 litre (l)

Imperial units
Imperial units used to be the standard measurements in Britain. You are most likely to come across the following:

Length
12 inches (in) = 1 foot (ft)
3 feet (ft) = 1 yard (yd)
1760 yards = 1 mile

Area (square measure)
144 square inches = 1 square ft
9 square feet = 1 square yd

Mass (or weight)
16 ounces (oz) = 1 pound (lb)
14 pounds = 1 stone

Capacity
8 pints = 1 gallon (gal)

There are some more **tables of measurements** on page 191.

tabulate

If you tabulate some information you arrange it in a list or a **table**. It makes it easier for people to find the information that they want. (It sometimes makes it easier to remember it too.)

tally tallying

Tallying was an early way of counting. It didn't need number names or figures. A man could check the number of animals he had by putting down a stone or a stick as each one went past him. Another way of tallying was to cut notches in a stick. The number of animals would match the number of stones, sticks or notches. The numbers would tally.

Later, tally sticks were used for keeping accounts. A piece of wood would be marked across with notches to show the items on an account. Then it would be split down the middle so that each person could have a matching stick.

There are still times when tallying is useful – if people are counting deliveries from a lorry, for example, or collecting data for a survey.

Nowadays, though, we do it by jotting down lines on paper.

We do it this way:

We don't write the numbers down though, we just draw the 'sticks' like this:

It's easy to count all the fives afterwards. This would represent 17:

5 + 5 + 5 + 2

Tally chart

If you need to count numbers of different things it is a good idea to make a tally chart with a separate space for each sort of thing.

Getting to school	
walk	卌 ‖
cycle	‖
bus	‖‖
car	卌 卌

tens boundary

5 + 5 = 10

5 + 6 = 11.　It is 5 + 5 and 1 more.
　　　　　　　The number has crossed a tens boundary.

8 + 5 = 13.　It is 8 + 2 and 3 more.
　　　　　　　It has also crossed a tens boundary.

28 + 5 = 33.　It is 28 + 2 and 3 more.
　　　　　　　It has gone over a multiple of ten. It has also
　　　　　　　crossed a tens boundary, 30.

tenths boundary

```
            T U · t h
```
Remember　　　0 · 0 1　= 1 hundredth
　　　　　　　0 · 1　　= 1 tenth

0·01 + 0·09 = 0·1　　(We could write 0·10 if we wanted to.)
0·05 + 0·05 = 0·1
0·05 + 0·07 = 0·12　It is 0·05 + 0·05 and 0·02 more.
　　　　　　　　　　The number has gone over the tenths boundary.

0·15 + 0·07 = 0·22　This has also gone over a tenths boundary.

tessellate

If identical shapes fit
together without leaving
any gaps we say that
they tessellate.

  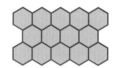

These shapes will not tessellate.

No matter how you arrange them,
there are gaps left in between them.

tetrahedron

A tetrahedron is a 3D shape with 4 faces.
A **regular** tetrahedron has an equilateral triangle for each face.
Look up **polyhedron** or **three-dimensional** if you want
more information about 3D shapes.

thousand

We write one thousand as 1000.

1000 = 10 x 100　　　　　A thousand thousands = one million.
1000 = 10 x 10 x 10　　　　　1000 x 1000 = 1 000 000

a
b
c
d
e
f
g
h
i
j
k
l
m
n
o
p
q
r
s
Tt
u
v
w
x
y
z

thousandth

One thousandth is $\frac{1}{1000}$

$\frac{1}{1000} = 0.001$

three-dimensional (3D)

Three-dimensional shapes have length and breadth and height. They are not 'flat' shapes like squares and triangles. The shapes that they form may be solid or hollow inside.

3D is short for three-dimensional. It is quicker to say – and it saves time when we are writing it. These are examples of 3D shapes:

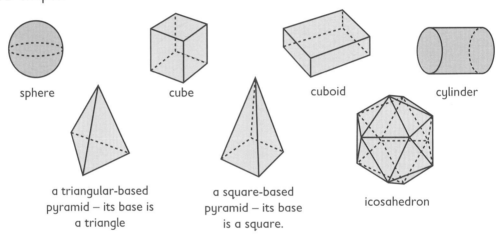

sphere   cube   cuboid   cylinder

a triangular-based pyramid – its base is a triangle

a square-based pyramid – its base is a square.

icosahedron

There is more information that might interest you under the headings of **polyhedron** and **prism**.

time

The first **time** we understand about is probably bedtime. Bit by bit time starts to get more important to us. We want to know things like, 'How long will it be to dinnertime?' 'How long is it to my birthday?' 'How long is it until playtime?'

We start to understand that today is the day we are in now. Yesterday was the day before today. Tomorrow hasn't come yet. It's the day after today.

Soon we need to know how long it takes to get to places and how long it takes to do things. We understand about being early for something and being late. Instead of days and hours we need to know about exact times, about minutes and even seconds. (Fractions of seconds can be important in a race!)

This table is a useful one to know:

> 60 seconds = 1 minute (min)
> 60 minutes = 1 hour (hr)
> 24 hours = 1 day
> 7 days = 1 week
> (14 days together are sometimes called a fortnight)
>
> 52 weeks = 1 year   10 years = 1 decade
> 12 months = 1 year   100 years = 1 century
> 365 days = 1 year   1000 years = 1 millennium
> 366 days = 1 leap year

(Look up **leap year** if you need to know more about it.)

In this section about time you can look up:
Telling the time
Midday, noon and midnight
am and pm
Fast and slow, gaining and losing
How long does it take?
A stopwatch
A timer
Time, distance and speed

In other parts of the book you can look up: **calendar,
century, dates, days of the week, leap year, month,
seasons, timetable,** and **twenty-four hour clock**.

Telling the time
There are lots of different kinds of clocks and watches.
Usually they show us the
time on a face like this,   or like this
(an **analogue clock**)   (a **digital clock**).

Both of these clocks are
showing the time as 10 o'clock.

Digital clocks and watches don't have hands that go round.
They usually show us the time using four digits. The first two
digits show the hour and the other two show the number of
minutes past the hour. (Some digital watches use 6 digits –
the last two show seconds.)
If you want to know more about this, look up **twenty-four
hour clock**.

More ...

time

Telling the time on an analogue clock
Look at this clock face.

It's a twelve hour clock.
The hands go round this way. (We call it clockwise.)
The shorter hand is the hour hand. The longer hand
is the minute hand.

The hour hand tells us what hour it is.
At 1 o'clock it points to 1. At 2 o'clock it points to 2. At 3
o'clock it points to 3 and so on.

It takes the hour hand a whole hour to move from one
number to the next. In 12 hours the hour hand goes all the
way round the clock face once.

The minute hand goes much faster. It moves from one number to the
next in five minutes. It goes all the way round the clock face in one
hour. In 12 hours the minute hand goes round 12 times.

If it is exactly
something o'clock
the minute hand
points to 12.

This shows 1 o'clock.   This shows 2 o'clock.   This shows 3 o'clock.
We can write 1:00.   We can write 2:00.   We can write 3:00.

In a quarter of an hour the **minute hand** goes a quarter of the way
round the clock. A quarter of an hour is 15 minutes.

In a quarter of an
hour the **hour hand**
moves a quarter of
the way towards the
next number.

This shows quarter   This shows quarter   This shows quarter
past 1.   past 2.   past 3.
We can write 1:15.   We can write 2:15.   We can write 3:15.

In half an hour the minute
hand goes half-way
round the clock. Half
an hour is 30 minutes.
In half an hour the hour
hand goes half-way
from one number
to the next.

This shows half past 1.   This shows half past 2.   This shows half past 3.
We can write 1:30.   We can write 2:30.   We can write 3:30.

These clock faces show some of the 'in between' times.

This shows 10 o'clock. We can write 10:00.

This shows 5 minutes past 10. We can write 10:05.

This shows 10 minutes past 10. We can write 10:10.

This shows 15 minutes past 10. It is a quarter of an hour past 10 o'clock. We can call it quarter past 10 or ten-fifteen. We usually write 10:15.

This shows 20 minutes past 10. We can write 10:20.

This shows 25 minutes past 10. We can write 10:25.

This shows 30 minutes past 10. It is half an hour past 10 o'clock. We can call it half past ten or ten-thirty. We usually write 10:30.

When the minute hand has gone more than half-way round the clock face it starts coming up towards the next hour. We can say it is so many minutes **past** the hour or it is so many minutes **to** the next hour.

This shows 35 minutes past ten. We write 10:35. We can also call it twenty-five to eleven. It is 25 minutes before 11 o'clock.

This shows 40 minutes past 10. We write 10:40. We can also call it twenty to eleven. It is 20 minutes before 11 o'clock.

This shows 45 minutes past 10. We write 10:45. We can also call it quarter to eleven. It is a quarter of an hour (15 minutes) before 11.

This shows 50 minutes past 10. We write 10:50. We can also call it ten to eleven. It is 10 minutes before 11.

This shows 55 minutes past ten. We write 10:55. We can also call it five to eleven. It is 5 minutes before 11.

a b c d e f g h i j k l m n o p q r s **Tt** u v w x y z

More ...

a
b
c
d
e
f
g
h
i
j
k
l
m
n
o
p
q
r
s

Tt

u
v
w
x
y
z

Midday and midnight
Midday is at 12 o'clock in the middle of the day.
It is sometimes called 12 noon.
Midnight is 12 o'clock at night.

am and pm
10am means 10 o'clock in the morning.
10pm means 10 o'clock in the evening.

If you want to change a pm time to a time on the 24-hour clock, look up **twenty-four hour clock**.

Fast and slow, gaining and losing
We say a clock or a watch is **gaining** if it is working too quickly.

If it showed the time as 9:30 when it was only 9:25 we would say it was 5 minutes **fast**. It was 5 minutes ahead of the real time. We would have to count back 5 minutes to find out the real time.

If we were told that a clock was 20 minutes fast we would know that it was 20 minutes ahead of the real time. We would have to count back 20 minutes to find out the real time. If it showed the time as 8:40 the real time would be 8:20.

We say a clock or a watch is **losing** time if it is working too slowly. If it showed the time as 6:15 when it was really 6:20 we would say it was 5 minutes **slow**. It was 5 minutes behind the real time.

If we were told that a clock was 20 minutes slow we would know that it was 20 minutes behind the real time. We would have to count on 20 minutes to find out the real time. If it showed the time as 6:05 the real time would be 6:25.

How long does it take?
We often need to know how long it is from one time to another. How long does a television programme last? How long has a cake been in the oven? How long will it take to get from one place to another?
Here are some examples.

1 *A programme starts at 5:10 pm. It ends at 5:35 pm. How long does it last?*

We could count on from 5:10 to 5:35.
5:10 to 5:20 = 10 mins
5:20 to 5:30 = 10 mins
5:30 to 5:35 = 5 mins
Altogether 5:10 to 5:35 = 25 mins

The answer is 25 minutes.

2 *A cake was put in the oven at 10:15 am. It is now:11:45am. How long has it been in the oven?*

We could count on like this:
10:15 to 11:15 = 1 hr
11:15 to 11:45 = 30 mins (or $\frac{1}{2}$ hr)

The answer is 1 hr 30 mins or $1\frac{1}{2}$ hrs.

3 *A journey starts at 10:05am and finishes at 2:30 pm. How long does it take?*

We could count on from 10:05am to 2:30pm.
10:05 to 11:05 = 1 hour
11:05 to 12:05 = 1 hour
12:05 to 1:05 = 1 hour
1:05 to 2:05 = 1 hour
2:05 to 2:30 = 25 minutes

Altogether the journey takes 4 hrs 25 mins.

A stopwatch
Short amounts of time are measured in seconds or even smaller units such as milliseconds. Some watches have an extra hand which measures seconds. That may be good enough, but sometimes a stopwatch is better. A stopwatch can be started and stopped very quickly and its face is clearly marked in seconds and fractions of a second. Stopwatches are often used for timing races.

A timer
Some timers can be set to buzz or ring after a certain time. A lot of cookers have one of these.
Some timers can be set to start something going at one time and stop at another. Video recorders have a timer that can be set to record a programme while you are out or watching another channel.

More ...

a
b
c
d
e
f
g
h
i
j
k
l
m
n
o
p
q
r
s
Tt
u
v
w
x
y
z

a
b
c
d
e
f
g
h
i
j
k
l
m
n
o
p
q
r
s
Tt
u
v
w
x
y
z

Time, distance and speed

Speed is often measured in kilometres per hour (km/h) or in metres per second. Miles per hour (mph) are also used.

If a cyclist travelled at 30 km/h, he would travel 30 kilometres in every hour.
60 kilometres would take 2 hours.
90 kilometres would take 3 hours.
15 kilometres would take $\frac{1}{2}$ hour (15 = $\frac{1}{2}$ of 30).

If a car travelled at an average speed of 40 mph (miles per hour), how long would it take for a journey of 100 miles?

40 miles takes 1 hr.
80 miles would take 2 hrs.
20 more miles would make up the 100 miles.
20 miles would take $\frac{1}{2}$ hr.
100 miles would take $2\frac{1}{2}$ hrs.

You might find it helpful to look up **speed** and **distance.**

Time

When we think about time we usually think about clocks and watches. Time is not just the passing of hours, minutes and seconds. It can be about the passing of days, weeks, months, years and centuries.

---

times

Times can mean times on clocks or times on timetables or the number of times that something is done.
When people say 'times' they often mean 'multiplied by.'
The sign for that is **x**.

To find 5 times 2 we multiply.
5 times 2 means 5 x 2
5 x 2 = 10

If Sara has £4 and Alex has three times as much, Alex has 3 x £4. Alex has £12.

Instead of two times we often say **twice.** If Petra has twice as much as Alex, Petra has 2 x £12
Petra has £24.

Someone may ask how many times one number will divide into another. For example, how many times will 5 divide into 15? (The answer is 3.)

You may want to look up **multiplication**, **division**, **time** (for telling the time) or **timetable**.

timetable

Timetables are lists of times which tell us when something happens. A school timetable shows the times when different lessons start and stop.

Most timetables are to do with travelling and most of them use the twenty-four hour clock.

24-hour clock times use four digits. The first two are hours. The last two are minutes. After 12:00 midday, the hours carry on 13:00 14:00 15:00 and so on until they get to midnight.

This means that 1am is written as 01:00 and 1pm is written as 13:00. You are not so likely to muddle up a morning time with an afternoon time – that's why it's used for timetables.

(If you have forgotten about this look up **twenty-four hour clock**.)

Here is part of a train timetable:

This shows us the times that trains leave Castleton and the times they arrive at Dunsford.
If we want to we can work out how long each train takes. Look at the timetable.

Castleton	Dunsford
depart	*arrive*
10:35	12:40
13:20	15:45
17:35	19:45

1 The first train:
10:35 to 11:35 to 12:35 = 2 hrs
12:35 to 12:40 = 5 mins
The 10:35 train takes 2 hrs 5 mins.

2 The second train:
13:20 to 14:20 to 15:20 = 2 hrs
15:20 to 15:45 = 25 mins.
The 13:20 train takes 2 hrs 25 mins.

3 The third train:
17:35 to 18:35 to 19:35 = 2 hrs
19:35 to 19:45 = 10 mins.
The 17:35 train takes 2 hrs 10 mins.

The 10:35 train is the fastest – it only takes 2 hours 5 minutes. It is faster than either of the others.

The 13:20 train is the slowest. It takes 2 hours 25 minutes. It is slower than either of the others.

The 17:35 train takes 2 hours 10 minutes. It is nearly as fast as the 10:35 train.

More ...

timetable

This timetable is arranged differently:

Whiteway	*depart*	10:25	11:25	12:25
Wolford		11:45	12:45	—
Barringdon	*arrive*	13:15	14:15	15:00

The first train leaves Whiteway at 10:25.
It stops at Wolford at 11:45.
It arrives at Barringdon at 13:15.

The second train leaves Whiteway at 11:25.
It stops at Wolford at 12:45.
It arrives at Barringdon at 14:15.

The third train leaves Whiteway at 12:25.
It does not stop at Wolford.
It arrives at Barringdon at 15:00 (3pm).

If you want to go to Barringdon the 12:25 train is the quickest
train – but it's no good if you want to go to Wolford!

Remember the fastest train – or bus – takes the shortest
time. It gets to its destination more quickly than the others.
The slowest train – or bus – takes the longest time. It gets
to its destination more slowly than the others.

> **Useful words to remember:**
> arrive   arrival   depart   departure
> destination (the place that someone is going to)

tonne

A tonne is a metric measure of mass or weight.

(Look up **mass** if you are not sure about this.)

1 tonne (t) = 1000 kilograms (kg)

total

The total is the whole of something. The total cost is the whole cost.

To find the total we count up – or add up – the whole lot.
We add to find:
– the total number
– the total weight
– the total amount
– the total population and so on.

translation

In maths a translation is about moving a shape in a certain way. You can slide a shape along – or up – or down – just as it is, but you can't turn it round so that it faces a different way and you can't stretch it or change its shape in any way.

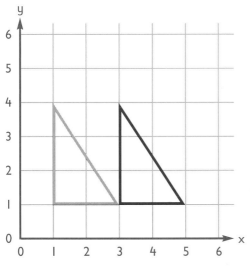

This shape has moved right.

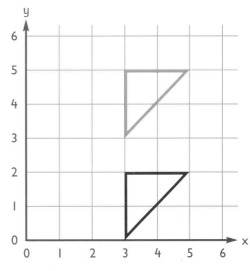

This shape has moved down.

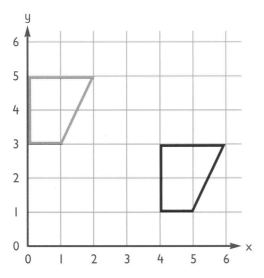

This shape has moved down and right.

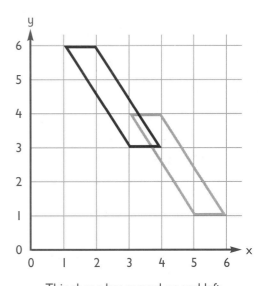

This shape has moved up and left.

trapezium

A trapezium is a 2D shape with 4 straight sides. 2 of its sides are parallel.

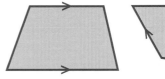 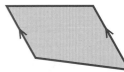

a
b
c
d
e
f
g
h
i
j
k
l
m
n
o
p
q
r
s
Tt
u
v
w
x
y
z

triangle

A triangle is a 2D shape with 3 straight sides and 3 angles.
The 3 angles in a triangle add up to 180°.

A right-angled triangle has an angle of 90°
(90° is a right angle). The longest side is
opposite the right angle. It is called the
hypotenuse. A right-angled triangle may be
isosceles or scalene.

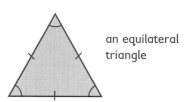
a right-angled
scalene triangle

An equilateral triangle has 3 sides of
equal length. It also has 3 equal angles.
Each angle measures 60° .

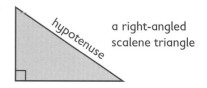
an equilateral
triangle

An isosceles triangle has 2 equal sides.
The angles opposite these 2 sides are
also equal.

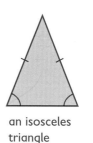
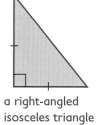

an isosceles
triangle

a right-angled
isosceles triangle

A scalene triangle has **no** equal sides
or angles. All 3 sides of a scalene triangle
are of different lengths. The angles are all
different too.

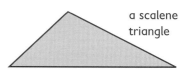
a scalene
triangle

Congruent triangles

Congruent triangles are exactly the same
size and shape as each other.

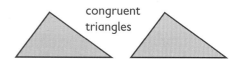
congruent
triangles

To find the **perimeter of a triangle** add up the lengths of
all its sides.

To find the **area of a right-angled triangle**:
Look at this right-angled triangle. It is half of a rectangle.
The area of the triangle will be half the area of the
rectangle.

The area of this rectangle is 6 cm x 4 cm = 24 cm²
The area of the triangle is half the area of the rectangle.
Half of 24 cm² = 12 cm²

triangular numbers

A triangular number can be shown by a triangle of dots.

1	3	6	10	15

1 is counted as a triangular number.
The next is 3, then 6, 10, 15, 21 and so on.

If you look at the sequence of triangular numbers you can
see how it is built up.

(1 + 2 = 3   3 + 3 = 6   6 + 4 = 10   10 + 5 = 15 and so on)

If you look at the patterns of dots again you will see why.

triangular prism

A prism is a special kind of 3D shape. Its two ends are exactly the same
size and shape and they are parallel to each other. A triangular prism
is shaped like a triangle all the way through its length.

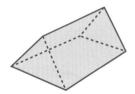 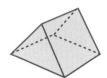

If you slice through a triangular prism parallel to one of its ends, the
new ends will be triangles too. The old ends and the new ends will
match exactly.

triangular pyramid

A triangular pyramid is a pyramid that has a triangle as its base.

 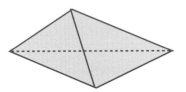

(A square pyramid has a square for a base.)

twice

Twice means two times.
If you do something twice you do it once and then you do it
one more time.
Twice three means two times three. 2 x 3 = 6

a
b
c
d
e
f
g
h
i
j
k
l
m
n
o
p
q
r
s
Tt
u
v
w
x
y
z

twenty-four hour clock

Most timetables use the 24-hour clock. Instead of counting the time up to 12:00 midday, then up to twelve again, the time is counted straight through the twenty-four hours from midnight on one day to midnight on the next.

12hr clock/24-hour clock			12hr clock/24-hour clock		
1am	=	01:00	1pm	=	13:00
2am	=	02:00	2pm	=	14:00
3am	=	03:00	3pm	=	15:00
4am	=	04:00	4pm	=	16:00
5am	=	05:00	5pm	=	17:00
6am	=	06:00	6pm	=	18:00
7am	=	07:00	7pm	=	19:00
8am	=	08:00	8pm	=	20:00
9am	=	09:00	9pm	=	21:00
10am	=	10:00	10pm	=	22:00
11am	=	11:00	11pm	=	23:00
12 o'clock midday (noon) = 12:00			12 o'clock midnight = 24:00		

Remember: From 12 o'clock midnight to 12 o'clock midday are **am** times.
From 12 o'clock midday to 12 o'clock midnight are **pm** times.

It's not so easy to muddle up a morning time with an afternoon time if you use the 24-hour clock.

24-hour clock times are always written using four figures. The first two show the hour. The last two show the minutes.

Digital clocks show midnight as 00:00

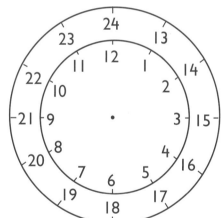

00:01 would be 1 minute after midnight. (The first minute of the new morning.)

00:30 would be 30 minutes after midnight.
01:30 would be 1:30am.
10:45 would be 10:45am.
13:30 would be 1:30pm.
15:27 would be 3:27pm.

The quick way to change times on the 24-hour clock to 'ordinary' times is to take 12 away from the hours. (You only need to do this for times from 13:00 to 24:00 of course.) The quick way to change pm times to 24-hour clock times is to add 12 to the hour.

two-dimensional (2D)

Two-dimensional shapes are flat shapes.
They have length and breadth (width) but no thickness.
Some 2D shapes have special names.
Here are some examples of them.

square

rectangle

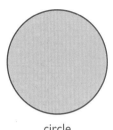
circle

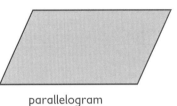
parallelogram

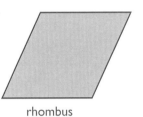
rhombus

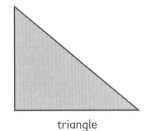
triangle

kite

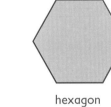
hexagon

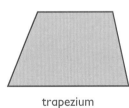
trapezium

star

oval

heptagon

a
b
c
d
e
f
g
h
i
j
k
l
m
n
o
p
q
r
s
Tt
u
v
w
x
y
z

a
b
c
d
e
f
g
h
i
j
k
l
m
n
o
p
q
r
s
t
Uu
v
w
x
y
z

unequal sharing

When we talk about sharing things we usually mean sharing them equally or dividing them up into equal groups. Sometimes we need to share things out differently.
Look at these examples.

Share 50p between Jan and Yvonne so that Jan has 10p more than Yvonne.

1 Give Jan her extra 10p.

Jan	Yvonne
10p	

2 Find out what's left.
50p − 10p = 40p

3 Share out what's left in the usual way.
40p ÷ 2 = 20p
They would each have 20p.

Jan	Yvonne
10p + 20p = 30p	20p

4 Jan has her 20p + the extra 10p.
Jan has 30p altogether.
Yvonne has 20p.
This uses up the 50p and Jan has 10p more than Yvonne.

A ruler and a pencil together cost £1. The ruler cost 50p more than the pencil. How much did they cost separately?

1 Put the extra 50p on one side for the ruler.

Ruler	Pencil
50p	

2 Find out how much is left.
£1 − 50p = 50p

3 Share out whatever is left in the usual way.
50p ÷ 2 = 25p
Put out 25p each.

Ruler	Pencil
50p + 25p = 75p	25p

4 The ruler would cost
50p + 25p = 75p
The pencil would cost 25p.
That comes to £1 altogether – and the ruler does cost 50p more than the pencil.

Divide 7 apples between 2 boys so that one has 3 less than the other.

1 If one has 3 less, then give the other one 3 to start with.

Boy A	Boy B
	3

2 Find out how many are left: $7 - 3 = 4$

3 Share out whatever is left in the usual way.
$4 \div 2 = 2$
They would have 2 each.

Boy A	Boy B
2	3 + 2 = 5

4 One boy could have 2 apples. The other boy could have 5 apples. (This uses up the 7 apples altogether and one boy does have 3 less than the other.)

There are other kinds of unequal sharing: such as when one person is paid three times as much as another. There is an example of this under **proportion**.

units boundary

Remember:
H T U·t

$\quad\quad 0 \cdot 1 \ = 1$ tenth

$\quad\quad 1 \cdot 0 \ = 1$ unit

$0 \cdot 1 + 0 \cdot 9 = 1$ (We could write $1 \cdot 0$ if we wanted to.)

$0 \cdot 5 + 0 \cdot 7 = 1 \cdot 2$
It is $0 \cdot 5 + 0 \cdot 5$ (making 1) and $0 \cdot 2$ more.
The number has gone over the units boundary.

$0 \cdot 8 + 0 \cdot 6 = 1 \cdot 4$
It is $0 \cdot 8 + 0 \cdot 2$ and $0 \cdot 4$ more.
This number has also crossed the units boundary.

a
b
c
d
e
f
g
h
i
j
k
l
m
n
o
p
q
r
s
t
Uu
v
w
x
y
z

a
b
c
d
e
f
g
h
i
j
k
l
m
n
o
p
q
r
s
t
u
Vv
w
x
y
z

value

To find the value of something you have to find out what it's worth. The value of 5 x 10p is 50p. The value of 3 + 5 = 8. If things are equal in value they are worth the same. 100p has the same value as £1 for example. 100p = £1.

When we multiply something by 1 its value doesn't change. It is still worth the same.

$4 \times 1 = 4$

$£10 \times 1 = £10$

$\frac{1}{2} \times 1 = \frac{1}{2}$

In a list of things, the one with the greatest value is worth the most. The one with the least value is worth less than any of the others.

The maximum value of something is the highest possible value it can have. The minimum value is its lowest possible value.

Venn diagrams

Venn diagrams are useful for sorting out groups of things – or groups of people. They are sometimes called **ring pictures**.

Look at this one. You can quickly see that Sanjay, Chris and Lucy play in a band and Mike, Helena and Jo are in a choir. Lisa and Zia are in both rings. They play in a band and they sing in a choir as well so the rings overlap.

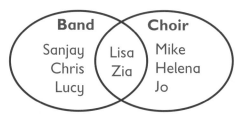

Look at this example. This Venn diagram was used to sort out a list of numbers into multiples of 3 and multiples of 5 and numbers which weren't either of these. This was the list of numbers:

12   20   2   9   15   10   4   25

The Venn diagram looked like this:

12 and 9 are multiples of 3.

10, 20 and 25 are multiples of 5.

15 = 3 x 5. It is a multiple of 3 and it is a multiple of 5 so it has to be in both rings. It goes where the rings overlap.

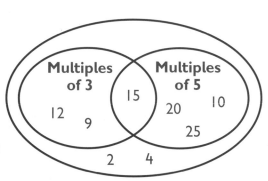

2 and 4 are not multiples of 3 or 5 so they are not in either of those rings.

vertex vertices *(The plural of vertex is vertices.)*

(Say 'verti-seez'.) A vertex is a corner point of a
polygon or a polyhedron. (It can also mean the
top or tip: the point furthest away from the base.)

 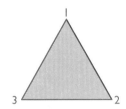 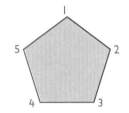 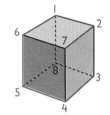

Another word for the highest point − or the tip − is the
apex. The tip of a cone can be called its apex.

vertical

Vertical means exactly upright.

A vertical line would be at right angles to a
horizontal line. (This is also called perpendicular.)
A set square is useful for checking this.

A door must be fixed vertically into its
door frame or it won't close properly.
(You might want to look up **horizontal** as well.)

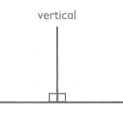

volume

Volume is the amount of space that something takes up.

Look at this example:
This cube is 1 cm long, 1 cm wide and 1 cm high.
It measures 1 cm x 1 cm x 1 cm.
We say its volume is 1 cubic centimetre.
We can write this as 1 cm^3.
It is the amount of space it takes up.

Suppose this cube is 3 cm long, 3 cm wide and 3 cm high.
It could be built up from 1 cm cubes.

Each layer would have
3 rows of cubes with
3 cubes in each row.
Each layer would need
3 x 3 = 9 cubes.

There would be 3 layers.
3 x 3 x 3 cubes would be needed altogether.
3 x 3 x 3 = 27
The volume of this cube would be 27 cm^3

More ...

To find the volume of any cube or cuboid we multiply the length by the breadth by the height. We can write *l x b x h* to save time. (Breadth is the same as width.)

Remember: all the measurements must be in the same units – they must all be a number of centimetres or all millimetres and so on.
The answer is always a **cubic** measure.
It could be m^3, cm^3 or mm^3.

This cuboid is 10 cm long, 5 cm wide and 2 cm high.

10 x 5 x 2 = 100
Its volume is 100 cm^3.

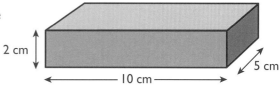

2 cm

5 cm

10 cm

weigh weight

(Say 'way' and 'wate'.) The weight of something is the amount that it weighs: it tells us how heavy it is.

A sack of potatoes is heavy. It would weigh a lot. The opposite of heavy is light. It's not always enough to know that something is heavy or light though. We usually need to know **how much** it weighs.

We use balances or scales to find the weight of something. We may use bathroom scales to weigh ourselves in kilograms. In the post office they use letter scales to weigh our letters in grams. We may use kitchen scales to weigh the things we need for cooking. In supermarkets we sometimes weigh the fruit and vegetables we want to buy.

In maths the word **mass** is used more often than weight. You may be told to 'measure the mass,' rather than 'find the weight.' (Look up **mass** if you want a reminder about this.) For everyday use the units of mass are used for weight. You can look them up on page 191.

width

(Say 'wit-th'.) Width is the measurement right across something from side to side. It tells us how wide it is. (It means the same as breadth.)

x-axis

The x-axis is the horizontal axis. (Remember: the **x** goes <u>**across**</u> !)

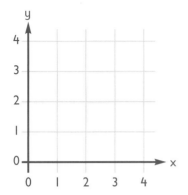

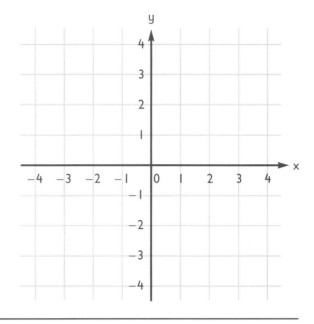

---

y-axis

The y-axis is the vertical axis.
The place where the x-axis and the y-axis cross each other
is called the origin.

---

yard

A yard is an imperial measure of length.

12 inches (in)	=	1 foot (ft)
3 feet	=	1 yard (yd)
1760 yds	=	1 mile

1 yard = 36 inches
1 metre is about 39 inches.

---

year

52 weeks	=	1 year
12 months	=	1 year
365 days	=	1 year (A leap year has 366 days.)

The seasons of the year are spring, summer, autumn and
winter.

The sections about **month**, **dates** or **leap year** might be
useful to you.

a
b
c
d
e
f
g
h
i
j
k
l
m
n
o
p
q
r
s
t
u
v
w
x
y
Zz

zero

The sign for zero is 0. It means none – not any.
0 can be a starting point in measuring or in counting on a
number line.

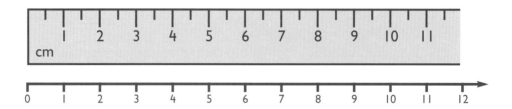

Numbers that are below zero – less than zero – have a
minus sign in front of them. We call them negative numbers.
Numbers above zero are positive numbers.

If we talk about the temperature being below zero we mean
it is below freezing point. It is below 0°C. (0 degrees on the
Celsius scale.)

If it is above zero it is above freezing point. (Above 0°C.)

(Look up **Celsius** if you want to know more about that.)

Zeros are very important in our number system. They help
to keep all the digits in the right places. You may find it
useful to look up **place value** or **decimals**.

Help yourself

On the next few pages you will find some suggestions for things you can try out in your spare time, as well as some quick reminders about tables, measurements and so on.

Things to practise and things to find out

- Ideas to try
- Test yourself
- Magic squares
- Tangram
- Roman numerals

Quick reminders

- Numbers
- Ordinal numbers
- Number bonds to 10
- Time
- Pounds (£) and pence
- Fractions, decimals and percentages
- Multiplication tables
- Multiplication square
- Tables of measurements

When you have a bit of spare time

- look up something that you aren't sure about
- practise things so that you can do them better – and perhaps more quickly
- try things out while you've got the time.

Here are some ideas that might be useful to you. (Have a pencil and some paper handy.)

doubling numbers

Jot down some numbers and then practise doubling them.
Check each answer carefully. If you halve an answer you should get back to the number you started with. If your number is 32 and you double it, your answer should be 64. Half of 64 is 32. (Look up **double** on page 59 if you need to.)
See if you can get quicker at halving and doubling without making mistakes. If you are really good at it give yourself some harder numbers to try.

calculator

Check the way you are using the calculator. Try out some easy things where you are sure that you know the answers. Then you can see if you are getting it right.
Look up **calculator** (pages 19 and 20) for some useful reminders.

mirror lines (reflective symmetry)

Draw some shapes. Draw the mirror lines on the shapes. (Remember, some shapes may not have any mirror lines at all.)

Check the lines you've drawn by using a mirror or by cutting out your shapes and folding along each line – one at a time. Check to see if you missed any.
Look up **mirror line** (pages 94/95) or **reflective symmetry** (page 138).

coins

Find some different ways of making up a pound from the coins we use.
Jot them down as you go along. (If you try to find them all it could take you longer than you expect!) There's a section about coins and money on pages 96/97 that might be useful to you.

directions

Could you tell a visitor the way from your classroom to – say – the school office? Write down the directions you would give them and draw a quick sketch. (Pages 50 and 51 might help you.)

plan

Draw a rough plan of your classroom. Try to get the shape right.
Mark in the positions of windows and doors, tables and desks.

measuring angles

Try measuring the angles shown on page 9. If you need help look up
protractor (pages 129-130).
If you need help to practise **drawing** angles look up page 131.
If you haven't already found it, the 'useful right angle' (p141) might
interest you.

divisibility tests

372   4109   49527
Which of these numbers can be exactly divided by 3?

Can any of them be divided exactly by 2 ..... or by 5 ..... or by 9 .....?
The divisibility tests give very quick ways of finding out. It's worth
knowing them. Look up pages 53 and 54. Jot down some more numbers
and try them out.

tables of measurements

Check up on the measurements that you use in your class work. (There
are some lists of measurements at the back of this book.) Remember
though, if you write down a few that you want to learn you must be very,
very careful not to make a mistake when you are copying them.

convert

You might want to look up **convert** to remind you about changing pence
to pounds, millimetres to centimetres, centimetres to metres and so on.

multiplication tables

Check up on the tables that you use in your class work. There are
some lists of multiplication tables on page 190. These are useful for
checking up on something you're not sure about – but it saves you a
lot of time when you really know them yourself.

If you need to look something up jot it down on a piece of paper when
you have a bit of spare time. Write it on one side of the paper and put
the answer on the back so you can test yourself from time to time.
Do make sure you put the right answer down though!

Try something different

Look in the contents list near the beginning of this book. Find something
you're not sure about or something that interests you.

Now try some of these

Some of them may be about things you haven't done yet. Just pick out the ones you think you know about. You can check your own answers. (It will help you to find your way around this book too!) Have a pencil and some paper handy. Remember – try first and then check.

angles
Do you know their names and sizes? Jot down the ones you remember then check your answers on pages 9 and 10.

triangles
What do you know about an equilateral triangle? Jot down everything you can think of. Look up page 61 to see if you're right about each thing – and if you can add anything else to your list.

quadrilaterals
What is a quadrilateral? Can you think of the names for 7 different kinds of quadrilaterals? Jot down as many as you can. What else do you know about them? Jot down what you know about each one. (Check your answers on pages 132 and 133. There is more information under their own headings.)

numbers
Which is the next number after one hundred? Which is the next after one thousand? Write your answers in numbers. (Check on page 116.)

milli-
How many words can you think of that start with **milli-**... ? (Look on page 93.)

polygon
What is a polygon? Draw one and label it. (Check on page 118.)

polygon and polyhedron
What is the difference between a polygon and a polyhedron? (Check on pages 118 and 119.)

ordinal numbers
Write down three ordinal numbers. (See page 188.)

compass
North and South are two **points of the compass**. Can you name any more? (Check on page 28.)

horizontal
Draw a horizontal line. Could you draw a vertical line? Look up pages 78/79 & 177 to see if you are right.

signs and symbols
Make a list of the signs and symbols that **you** use in maths. Write down what each one stands for. Now look up page 149 to see if you got them right. If you remembered all the ones that you use you might be interested to find out about a few more.

oblong
How many lines of symmetry does an oblong have? (See page 104.)

Venn diagram
What is a Venn diagram used for? (See page 176.)

time, distance and speed
If a car travelled at an average speed of 40 mph how long would it take for a journey of 100 miles? (Look on page 166.)

percentages
What does per cent mean? Write $\frac{20}{100}$ as a percentage. What is 10% of £20? What is 5% of £40? (Check percentages on pages 111-113.)

order
What does ascending order mean? Put these fractions into ascending order:
$3\frac{1}{4}$ $\frac{3}{4}$ $\frac{1}{2}$ $2\frac{1}{2}$ $\frac{1}{4}$ (See pages 106 and 107.)

factor
Find a common factor of 12 and 15. (Look up page 64.)

square numbers
Which of these are **square** numbers 2 4 6 8 9 12 16 ?
(Check up on page 152.)

parallel lines
What is special about parallel lines? (Look up on page 109.)

perimeter
What's the perimeter of a rectangle that's 15 cm wide and 10 cm long?
(Page 113 will help you check this answer.)

fractions
Add $\frac{1}{4} + \frac{1}{4} + \frac{1}{4}$ (page 66)   Subtract $\frac{4}{6}$ from $\frac{5}{6}$ (page 70)

Change $2\frac{7}{8}$ to an improper fraction.   Reduce $\frac{18}{3}$ to its lowest terms.

(There is a lot of information about fractions on pages 66 to 71.)

equivalent
What does equivalent mean? (Check on page 61 – and on 69 for equivalent fractions.)

Magic squares

Of course there is nothing really magic about these squares but a lot of people find them interesting! In a 'magic square' the numbers in every row, column and diagonal add up to the same total.

a row

a column

a diagonal

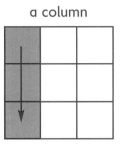
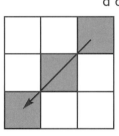
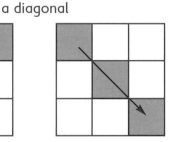

Now look at these squares. In the first one every row, column, and diagonal adds up to 15. In the second they all add up to 18. Check them and see.

6	1	8
7	5	3
2	9	4

9	2	7
4	6	8
5	10	3

12	5	10
7	9	11
8	13	6

What do the rows, columns and diagonals add up to in the third square?
Could you make a 'magic square' like these with a 7 in the middle?
Try making some more 'magic squares' like these. You can make bigger ones too – as long as they have an odd number of rows and columns.

Tangram

A tangram is a square that has been cut into 7 pieces in a special way to make a puzzle. When the pieces are mixed up it can be quite tricky to put them back into a square! These tangram pieces have been arranged to make a different shape.

If you have a tangram puzzle at home or in your class, can you fit the pieces together to make up the square?

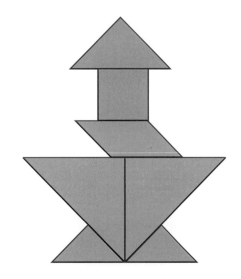

Roman numerals are still used sometimes on clocks or to show dates. This list shows the Roman numerals with the numbers we normally use underneath them. (Sometimes you may see IIII on a clock face instead of IV.)

I	II	III	IV	V	VI	VII	VIII	IX	X
1	2	3	4	5	6	7	8	9	10

XI	XII	XIII	XIV	XV	XVI	XVII	XVIII	XIX	XX
11	12	13	14	15	16	17	18	19	20

L	C	D	M
50	100	500	1000

Remember:
V = 5
IV is 1 before 5.   IV = 4
VI is 1 after 5.   VI = 6

When Romans wrote down their numbers they put them in order with the largest first.

MD   = 1500 (1000 and 500)
MDCL   = 1650 (1000 + 500 + 100 + 50)
MDCLXVI   = 1666 (1000 + 500 + 100 + 50 + 10 + 5 + 1)

The only time you will see a smaller number **before** a larger number is when it has to be taken away.

L   = 50
XL   = 40 (10 before 50 or 10 less than 50)
CXL   = 140 (100 and 10-before-50)
CLX   = 160 (100 and 50 and 10)
MCM   = 1900 (1000 and 100-before-1000) = 1000 and 900
MCMXCIX   = 1999
MM   = 2000
MMII   = 2002

Numbers

Numbers and number names

1	one
2	two
3	three
4	four
5	five
6	six
7	seven
8	eight
9	nine
10	ten
11	eleven
12	twelve
13	thirteen
14	fourteen
15	fifteen
16	sixteen
17	seventeen
18	eighteen
19	nineteen
20	twenty
21	twenty-one
30	thirty
31	thirty-one
40	forty
41	forty-one
50	fifty
51	fifty-one
60	sixty
61	sixty-one
70	seventy
71	seventy-one
80	eighty
81	eighty-one
90	ninety
91	ninety-one
100	one hundred (a hundred)
101	one hundred and one
150	one hundred and fifty
200	two hundred
1000	one thousand
10 000	ten thousand
100 000	one hundred thousand
1 000 000	one million

Ordinal numbers

1st	first
2nd	second
3rd	third
4th	fourth
5th	fifth
6th	sixth
7th	seventh
8th	eighth
9th	ninth
10th	tenth
11th	eleventh
12th	twelfth
13th	thirteenth
14th	fourteenth
15th	fifteenth
16th	sixteenth
17th	seventeenth
18th	eighteenth
19th	nineteenth
20th	twentieth
21st	twenty-first
30th	thirtieth
40th	fortieth
50th	fiftieth
60th	sixtieth
70th	seventieth
80th	eightieth
90th	ninetieth
100th	hundredth
101st	hundred and first

Number bonds to 10

$$0 + 10 = 10$$
$$1 + 9 = 10$$
$$2 + 8 = 10$$
$$3 + 7 = 10$$
$$4 + 6 = 10$$
$$5 + 5 = 10$$
$$6 + 4 = 10$$
$$7 + 3 = 10$$
$$8 + 2 = 10$$
$$9 + 1 = 10$$
$$10 + 0 = 10$$

Time

60 seconds	= 1 minute
60 minutes	= 1 hour
24 hours	= 1 day
7 days	= 1 week
365 days	= 1 year
366 days	= 1 leap year
52 weeks	= 1 year
12 months	= 1 year
10 years	= 1 decade
100 years	= 1 century
1000 years	= 1 millennium

Fractions

If we need to find $\frac{1}{2}$ of something we divide it by 2.

If we need to find $\frac{1}{3}$ of something we divide it by 3.

If we need to find $\frac{1}{4}$ of something we divide it by 4.

If we need to find $\frac{1}{5}$ of something we divide it by 5 and so on.

To find $\frac{2}{3}$ of something, find $\frac{1}{3}$ of it then multiply by 2.

To find $\frac{5}{6}$ of something, find $\frac{1}{6}$ of it then multiply by 5.

To find $\frac{9}{10}$ of something, find $\frac{1}{10}$ of it then multiply by 9.

Money: (£) pound

100p = £1.00	20p = £0.20 = £$\frac{1}{5}$
75p = £0.75 = £$\frac{3}{4}$	10p = £0.10 = £$\frac{1}{10}$
50p = £0.50 = £$\frac{1}{2}$	5p = £0.05 = £$\frac{1}{20}$
25p = £0.25 = £$\frac{1}{4}$	1p = £0.01 = £$\frac{1}{100}$

One pound fifty pence is written as £1.50
One pound five pence is written as £1.05

Decimals

These are useful decimals to learn:

0·75	= $\frac{3}{4}$	0·2	= $\frac{1}{5}$ ($\frac{1}{5} = \frac{2}{10}$)
0·5	= $\frac{1}{2}$	0·1	= $\frac{1}{10}$
0·25	= $\frac{1}{4}$	0·01	= $\frac{1}{100}$
0·125	= $\frac{1}{8}$		

Percentages

$100\% = \frac{100}{100}$

$50\% = \frac{50}{100} = \frac{1}{2}$ $25\% = \frac{25}{100} = \frac{1}{4}$ $75\% = \frac{75}{100} = \frac{3}{4}$

These are useful to know.

$75\% = \frac{3}{4}$	$33\frac{1}{3}\% = \frac{1}{3}$	$20\% = \frac{1}{5}$
$50\% = \frac{1}{2}$	$66\frac{2}{3}\% = \frac{2}{3}$	$10\% = \frac{1}{10}$
$25\% = \frac{1}{4}$		$5\% = \frac{1}{20}$
$12·5\%$ or $12\frac{1}{2}\% = \frac{1}{8}$		$1\% = \frac{1}{100}$

Multiplication tables

x2	x3	x4	x5	x6
1 x 2 = 2	1 x 3 = 3	1 x 4 = 4	1 x 5 = 5	1 x 6 = 6
2 x 2 = 4	2 x 3 = 6	2 x 4 = 8	2 x 5 = 10	2 x 6 = 12
3 x 2 = 6	3 x 3 = 9	3 x 4 = 12	3 x 5 = 15	3 x 6 = 18
4 x 2 = 8	4 x 3 = 12	4 x 4 = 16	4 x 5 = 20	4 x 6 = 24
5 x 2 = 10	5 x 3 = 15	5 x 4 = 20	5 x 5 = 25	5 x 6 = 30
6 x 2 = 12	6 x 3 = 18	6 x 4 = 24	6 x 5 = 30	6 x 6 = 36
7 x 2 = 14	7 x 3 = 21	7 x 4 = 28	7 x 5 = 35	7 x 6 = 42
8 x 2 = 16	8 x 3 = 24	8 x 4 = 32	8 x 5 = 40	8 x 6 = 48
9 x 2 = 18	9 x 3 = 27	9 x 4 = 36	9 x 5 = 45	9 x 6 = 54
10 x 2 = 20	10 x 3 = 30	10 x 4 = 40	10 x 5 = 50	10 x 6 = 60

x7	x8	x9	x10
1 x 7 = 7	1 x 8 = 8	1 x 9 = 9	1 x 10 = 10
2 x 7 = 14	2 x 8 = 16	2 x 9 = 18	2 x 10 = 20
3 x 7 = 21	3 x 8 = 24	3 x 9 = 27	3 x 10 = 30
4 x 7 = 28	4 x 8 = 32	4 x 9 = 36	4 x 10 = 40
5 x 7 = 35	5 x 8 = 40	5 x 9 = 45	5 x 10 = 50
6 x 7 = 42	6 x 8 = 48	6 x 9 = 54	6 x 10 = 60
7 x 7 = 49	7 x 8 = 56	7 x 9 = 63	7 x 10 = 70
8 x 7 = 56	8 x 8 = 64	8 x 9 = 72	8 x 10 = 80
9 x 7 = 63	9 x 8 = 72	9 x 9 = 81	9 x 10 = 90
10 x 7 = 70	10 x 8 = 80	10 x 9 = 90	10 x 10 = 100

A multiplication square

Look carefully at the numbers in this square. It is not the same as a 100 counting square. In this square you can find all of the answers to the multiplication tables shown above. It's a really neat way of showing them.

Suppose you want to know what 4 x 5 comes to.

Find 4 in the first column.
Then run your finger across the row until you get to column 5.
Then you can see that the answer is 20.
4 x 5 = 20

1	2	3	4	5	6	7	8	9	10
2	4	6	8	10	12	14	16	18	20
3	6	9	12	15	18	21	24	27	30
4	8	12	16	20	24	28	32	36	40
5	10	15	20	25	30	35	40	45	50
6	12	18	24	30	36	42	48	54	60
7	14	21	28	35	42	49	56	63	70
8	16	24	32	40	48	56	64	72	80
9	18	27	36	45	54	63	72	81	90
10	20	30	40	50	60	70	80	90	100

Metric units

Length
10 millimetres (mm) = 1 centimetre (cm)
100 centimetres (cm) = 1 metre (m)
1000 metres (m)   = 1 kilometre (km)

Mass
1000 milligrams (mg) = 1 gram (g)
1000 grams (g)   = 1 kilogram (kg)

Capacity
1000 millilitres (ml) = 1 litre (l)
100 centilitres (cl) = 1 litre

Area
100 square millimetres (mm^2)   = 1 square centimetre (cm^2)
10 000 square centimetres (cm^2) = 1 square metre (m^2)

Imperial units

Length
12 inches (in)   = 1 foot (ft)
3 feet (ft)   = 1 yard (yd)
36 inches   = 1 yard
1760 yards (yds) = 1 mile

Mass (or weight)
16 ounces (oz)   = 1 pound (lb)
14 pounds (lbs)   = 1 stone (st)

Capacity
8 pints (pts) = 1 gallon (gal)

Area (square measures)
144 square inches = 1 square foot
9 square feet   = 1 square yard

Approximate equivalents

Length
2·5 cm is about 1 inch
30 cm is about 1 foot
1 metre is about 39 inches
1 kilometre is about $\frac{5}{8}$ mile
8 km is about 5 miles.

Mass (or weight)
30 grams are about 1 ounce (oz)
28 grams is a bit nearer if you need to be more accurate.
1 kilogram is about 2·2 pounds (lbs)

Capacity
1 litre is about 1·75 pints
4·5 litres are about 1 gallon